WHAT IS IT ABOUT TEXAS?

Historical Stories About the Lone Star State

by

M. SCOTT SOSEBEE

STEPHEN F. AUSTIN STATE UNIVERSITY PRESS

Copyright © 2021 by Stephen F. Austin State University Press

Printed in the United States
All rights reserved.
First Edition

Production Manager: Kimberly Verhines
Book Design: Jerri Bourrous

IBSN: 978-1-62288-924-2

For more information:
Stephen F. Austin State University Press
P.O. Box 13007 SFA Station
Nacogdoches, Texas 75962
sfapress@sfasu.edu
www.sfasu.edu/sfapress
936-468-1078

Distributed by Texas A&M University Press Consortium
www.tamupress.com

CONTENTS

Introduction ix

SECTION I: PEOPLE

Exploring Texas on Two Fronts: Coronado and Moscoso / 1

A Borderlands Adventurer: Louis De St. Denis / 4

The Padre of Padre Island / 7

Texas Renaissance Man: Jose Antonio Navarro / 10

Texas' Soldier: Albert Sidney Johnston / 13

The Most Hated Man in Texas / 16

Doing the Best That He Could Under Trying Conditions: Norris Wright Cuney / 19

Waco's Baritone Maestro: Jules Bledsoe / 22

A Women's Rights Pioneer / 25

The First Country Star: Vernon Dalhart / 28

From Mess Attendant to Hero: Doris Miller and Pearl Harbor / 31

Distinguished Defiance: Dr. Hector P. Garcia and Tejano Rights / 34

Texas' Theater Auteur: Margo Jones / 37

The Texan Member of the "Big Four:" James L. Farmer, Jr. / 40

She Stood Up For What Was Right: Lulu Belle White / 43

A Very Different and Reluctant Cold Warrior: Van Cliburn / 46

Allan Shivers, the Tidelands, and the 1952 Governor's Race / 49

Cooley and Debakey: Two Innovative Surgeons Made Houston a "Heart" Capital / 52

Lee Harvey Oswald's "Other" Victim / 55

A Conversation With the Last Democratic Senator from Texas / 58

SECTION II: PLACES

The Road From the North: Trammel's Trace / 63

A Gateway to Texas / 66

Mexican Sentinel in East Texas: Fort Teran / 69

A Forgotten Town: Independence, TX / 72

A City Where the Decencies of Life Were Forgotten / 74

The Loneliest Outpost on the Frontier / 77

Swept Away: The Story of Indianola / 80

Mary Allen College: An Educational Beacon for African Americans / 83

Protecting The Gulf: Fort Crockett / 86

Keeping the Enemy in Texas: World War II POW Camps / 89

Ahead of Its Time: The Shamrock Hotel / 91

A Resting Place Fit for Texans: The Texas State Cemetery / 94

SECTION III: EVENTS

The Ill-Fated Matamoros Expedition / 99

Miscalculation and Bravery: The Battle of Coleto / 102

Sam and Santa Anna: The Day They Met / 105

Not Our Finest Hour: The Cherokee War of 1839 / 108

Lowering The Lone Star / 111

A Vision of Ruin: Sam Houston, Texas, and Secession / 114

Defending the Coast: The Battle of Galveston—1862 / 117

Patriots or Traitors?: German Unionists and the Battle / 119
    of the Nueces

Leaving Texas: The Exodus of 1879 / 122

Establishing Voting Barriers: From Poll Taxes to the / 125
    The All-White Primary

The Camp Logan Riot of 1917 / 128

A Shield Against Racism: The Founding of LULAC / 130

Commemorating Independence: The Building of the / 133
    San Jacinto Monument

It was a Terrible Roar: The New London School Explosion / 136

Changing Texas Politics After the War / 138

Massive Resistance," Texas, and the NAACP / 140

A Game that Was Not Just a Game / 143

A World's Fair in Texas: HemisFair '68 / 146

Greed and Scandal in the Legislature: The Sharpstown Incident / 149

SECTION IV: REFLECTION

The Five Most Transformative Events in Texas History: One / 155
    Man's List

A Struggle Just to Survive: African American Colleges in Texas / 167

A Texas Gift to the Nation: The Origins of Juneteenth / 170

A Texas Independence Day Tradition / 173

Do Fence Me In: Barbed Wire and the Texas Cattle Industry / 176

Baseball in Texas / 179

Casting a Hooded Shadow Across the Land: Texas / 181
    and the 2nd Ku Kux Klan

Cinco de Mayo and the "Texas Connection" / 184

Creating Their Own Space: Freedom Colonies / 186

Saving a Texas Shrine / 188

The Origin of Tex-Mex / 191

The Myth of Reconstruction in Texas / 193

The Sad Saga of Felix Longoria / 195

What Was Sam Houston's Ultimate Plan? / 197

Yes, We Were "Cowboys," Too / 200

For my Dad and Mom, Winston and Mary Sosebee

*I am grateful that you allowed me to pursue whatever made me happy,
and also loved history along with me*

Introduction

PEOPLE HAVE OFTEN ASKED ME, "Why did you become a historian?" That is a complex question to answer as I took a long, twisted path towards such a conclusion. Suffice to say, it was not my first career choice, nor was it even my second. But, eventually, one has to give up his childhood dreams—I realized early I would never be the next Mike Schmidt or Randy White—or even those adult choices that seemed right at the time but did not quite reach the heights or aspirations one thought they would at the time they were made. But, my path did eventually lead to what I truly believe I was born to do, and that is study, research, and write about the past.

Related to the above question, is one in which I can give a different answer. When I did make the decision to pursue the study of the past as a profession there was no question whatsoever that I would make Texas history my specialty. To a large extent, I was born to study Texas history. Both of my grandfathers loved to talk about history, and, of course, Texas history was what they were most drawn toward. When I was young, my dad loved to take car trips—I think we may have driven over every road in the state, and certainly explored every nook and cranny of West Texas—and we never failed to stop at historical sites, places, and always read every Texas State Historical Marker we came across. I became fascinated with all aspects of the state's past, and even when I was pursuing other careers and ambitions, I read Texas history books and articles, and learned as much as I could about Texas heritage.

My path to being a professional historian eventually meandered from graduate school at Texas Tech to a faculty position at Stephen F.

Austin State University in Nacogdoches. I do not think there could be a better place to be a Texas historian than in the oldest town in Texas. I was thrilled to be able to take such a job, but I was not prepared for the good fortune that would fall on me in such a short time after I arrived at SFA. Archie P. McDonald was one of those "names" that those of us in the profession just "know." He had been the Executive Director of the East Texas Historical Association for over thirty years, was a constant presence at historical conferences, and an in-demand speaker for meetings and functions throughout the state. Archie, however, had decided to retire, and through a series of very fortunate circumstances I was appointed as his successor.

Archie "took me under his wing" during the 2007-2008 academic year and showed me how to perform his duties, to prepare his retirement in August 2008. One of those obligations was writing a weekly history column that appeared in regional newspapers. He agreed that we would "share" the writing duties that first year, but that beginning in the fall semester of 2008 the whole kit and caboodle would be mine to write. So, I became a newspaper columnist and I found out that I enjoyed it. It was different writing than much I did, and still do, on the fully academic side, but being able to share stories and historical interpretation with a wide, more varied audience appealed to me. It also made me a better historian, and allowed me to expand on narratives about Texas' past, something that I relished doing.

I continue to write the weekly column, and as of May 2019 I counted that I had accumulated almost 600 columns about a myriad of Texas subjects. I also decided that it was time to put some of them in one source, an amalgam of those writings over various Texas topics. The collection in this book is meant to inform, entertain, and perhaps make one ponder how the state's past has developed and progressed. Maybe, out there, there is someone else who can read these and think "what is it about Texas" that makes one want to know more, just as I did decades ago as I started on that meandering avenue to the present. I hope that you enjoy reading what is here.

I. People

Exploring Texas on Two Fronts: Coronado and Moscoso

AFTER CHRISTOPHER COLUMBUS TRAVERSED the Atlantic in 1492 and made landfall in the Caribbean Sea, Spain embarked on a number of exploratory efforts in the New World. Eventually, within the next forty years the Iberian nation began to establish a presence in the New World, and established colonies on Cuba, Puerto Rico, Jamaica, Dominica, and the beginnings of its vast empire in Mexico (New Spain). From such bases, Spanish explorers began to map and make landings on the land mass that would eventually become the United States, mostly in a search for the same gold and silver riches they had found in Mexico.

One of those early expeditions was the ill-fated excursion led by Pánfilo de Narvàez in 1527-28. After landing in Florida near Sarasota Bay, storms and miscommunication caused Narvàez and about half his crew to be stranded in Florida when their ships left for Cuba without them. The stranded Spanish sailors made crude boats and took to the Gulf of Mexico with hopes that they could float along the coast line to Mexico. That did not happen. The group became marooned on San Luis Island just west of Galveston. A brutal winter and storms left only a few Spaniards alive (the fate of Narvàez is not clear), including the expedition's treasurer Àlvar Nùñez, Cabeza de Vaca Nùñez and his three cohorts spent years as captives of native tribes before making their way to Mexico in 1536 to tell their story.

The tale of a vast land north of New Spain piqued the interest of the Spanish viceroy in Mexico City. Spanish authorities became convinced that the northern frontier was full of riches, including the legendary seven cities of gold. The viceroy recruited Francisco Vàsquez de Coronado, a young nobleman hungry to become a *conquistador*, to lead a large expedition north into these lands. Coronado and his coterie marched north in 1540, bound for Zuni villages in present-day New Mexico in the land the Spaniards came to call *Cibola*, which was actually a Zuni word for bison. Earlier reports named these villages as "gleaming cities of gold," so Coronado pointed in that direction. When he arrived all he found were pueblo villages, and while they did cast a shine in the sunlight that was due to the quartz in their rock dwellings, not gold.

Determined to continue his quests—and after torturing the natives of the pueblos for information—the Zuni directed Coronado to the east. From the pueblos on the Rio Grande, he and his men marched across the *Llano Estacado*, through present-day Blanco Canyon, across the plains of what would become Texas, to end up at a small, impoverished Wichita village in current Kansas. Disillusioned, Coronado trudged back to Mexico City, his expedition a failure.

At approximately the same time that Àlvar Nùñez was arriving in Mexico City, another expedition authorized by another viceroy left Cuba bound for Florida, also seeking riches and conquest in the north. Hernando de Soto had first come to the New World with the new governor of Panama, and he participated in the Spanish conquest of Central America and Peru. After he learned of Juan Ponce de Leon's discoveries in Florida, de Soto, who had briefly returned to Spain, sailed to Cuba and then led an expedition of nine ships and over six hundred

Accompanying de Soto was Luis de Alvarado Moscoso, another veteran of the conquests of Peru and Central America. De Soto landed near present day Tampa in May 1539. Before they left the area they came across Juan Ortiz, a survivor of the Narvaez expedition. Ortiz had learned native languages and thus served as a guide and interpreter to the party. The Spaniards traveled north along the Gulf Coast, then on into Georgia, the Carolinas and Tennessee. After a turn back toward the Gulf for resupply from a ship from Cuba, the band made their way into present day Alabama where they encountered great resistance from the local natives. The ensuing battles against the Mobilian tribe cost the Spanish over two hundred men—and they slaughtered over two thousand of the Mobilian.

The wounded, sickly, disheartened Spaniards had found no gold and no great cities. They continued westward until they became the first documented Europeans to reach the Mississippi River in May 1541. Upon reaching the western bank, de Soto became ill and died—probably from pneumonia—and legend is that his men weighted his body and interred it in the Mississippi. Command of the troupe then passed to Moscoso.

Moscoso continued to lead the men west, now with survival and eventually reaching New Spain more important to them than finding riches and making conquests. As they marched they used native names to mark the places they passed. For example, as they passed through northwestern Louisiana they came to call the area "Naguatex," thus the eventual name of "Natchitoches," and after turning south from there they crossed the Sabine to come into contact with the Ais tribe of the Hasinai Caddo Confederacy, from whom they received favorable treatment.

They probably traveled as far west as the Brazos River, near present day Bryan, before they turned back, unsure if they could reach New Spain. They traveled back through East Texas, once again pausing with the Ais to replenish their exhausted food supply. The beleaguered Spaniards then returned to the site of de Soto's death, fashioned rafts, and floated down the Mississippi River and entered the Gulf of Mexico. The reduced party of now only about three hundred then hugged the coastline and sailed down the coasts of Louisiana and Texas and finally reached Mexico in the fall of 1543.

Like Coronado, Moscoso reported that the expedition was a failure. His account to the viceroy described the region as full of inhospitable weather, even more dangerous natives, and no signs of wealth. The only favorable story he provided was the friendliness of the Ais. As a result of these two audacious expeditions, Spain decided to forgo further exploration of the northern frontier, and would not return to what we now call Texas until well into the 1600s.

A Borderlands Adventurer: Louis De St. Denis

IMAGINE IF YOU CAN THAT YOU HAVE COME to live in a place that was completely isolated from almost every experience you have ever had in your life. You can barely communicate with any other humans with whom you come into contact, and the physical environment is dangerous to the point of potential death greeting you every day. Such was the life of Louis Juchereau De St. Denis, a Frenchman who lived in the wilds of French Louisiana on the border with Spanish Texas in the early 1700s. St. Denis would go on to be a primary actor in why the Spanish decided to make East Texas the first place they tried to settle in Texas.

When he was born in Quebec in 1674, Louis St. Denis became the eleventh of what would eventually be twelve children, not an easy lot in life now and even less so in the seventeenth century. His family was fairly well off in the New World and they sent the young boy off to finish his education in France, but St. Denis had been stricken with "New World fever," so, in 1699, St. Denis left France as part of the Sieur d'Iberville expedition bound for the newly opened French colony of Louisiana.

St. Denis became a prominent part of the administration of Louisiana. He commanded a fort on the Mississippi and in the new settlement at Biloxi. Eventually, he would be one of the first men to explore the region along the lower Red River, ascending all the way up that stream into present-day Arkansas and almost all the way to what would become Oklahoma. His journeys to the north of the primary French settlements along the Gulf made him the first Frenchman to chart trails and map what would become the state of Louisiana. It also allowed him to become aware of the native peoples living in the region, principally groups belonging to the Caddo Confederacy.

The Mississippi basin, which the French were then exploiting, had first been claimed by Spanish explorers in the early 1500s, but the Spanish authorities had generally ignored the northern reaches of their North American empire in favor of developing the valley of Mexico. That began to change in the 1680s when Robert Cavelier, Sieur de La Salle descended the Mississippi River out of the Great Lakes all the way to the mouth on the Gulf. He had claimed the entire drainage basin for the King of France, which is what had led St. Denis to come to the New World. La Salle's second journey into what he called Louisiana resulted in his landing in Texas, which greatly alarmed the Spanish authorities in Mexico City. Thus, they sent Alonso De Leon, along with Franciscan friar Father Massanet to found a mission and presidio to stop French incursions. As a result, Massanet founded Mission San Francisco de los Tejas in 1690, and De Leon established a nearby presidio. The mission struggled, and the French threat never materialized, and within a year the Spanish abandoned East Texas.

The Spanish Franciscans had always lamented the closing of the mission among the Caddo, so in 1713, another order priest, Francisco Hidalgo, hatched a bit of a scheme. He knew that St. Denis had made contacts among the natives in the Red River region, so he sent a letter to the French authorities in Mobile requesting that they—the Spanish rival—send spiritual advisors to the Indians on the northern frontier. Probably a little suspicious of Spanish intentions, the French governor sent not priests but the experienced explorer St. Denis to the north. St. Denis made contact with a band of Natchitoches Caddos living along the Red, made trade agreements, and set up a trading post in what would become Natchitoches, Louisiana, making it the first settlement in French Louisiana.

From there St Denis traveled to the lands of the Hasinai near present-day Nacogdoches, and eventually appeared at the Spanish outpost of San Juan Bautista on the Rio Grande near present-day Eagle Pass. The Spanish were naturally wary of a Frenchman in their territory and they arrested St. Denis, although he was not fully confined, just forbidden to leave the presidio. St. Denis then took some curious actions. Perhaps he really did do it for love. He began to court and eventually own the heart of the Spanish commander Diego Ramon's granddaughter. Eventually, St. Denis married his beau, declared his allegiance to the King of Spain, and came back to San Juan Bautista to serve in the King's Army.

More than likely with some coaxing from St. Denis, in 1716, Diego Ramon declared the Spanish intentions of reestablishing the missions in East Texas. Ramon left San Juan Bautista, and he took St. Denis with him. As part of a Spanish expedition, St. Denis' experience helped to pave the way for the eventual establishment of six missions in East Texas, including *Nuestra Senora de Guadalupe* in what would become Nacogdoches as well as the reestablishment of *San Francisco de los Tejas*.

European intrigue made Spain and France opponents once again in 1719, and St. Denis (his wife joined him in 1721) was forced to flee once again to Louisiana and Natchitoches. He became the French commander at the fort at the settlement he founded, and at various times he cooperated with the Spanish in East Texas, while at others he feuded with them. Louis St. Denis would eventually die at Natchitoches in 1744, but his legacy remained as the primary reason France was able to secure what would became the vast Louisiana territory, as well as a huge part of why Texas remained in Spanish hands, and why East Texas became the edge of the Spanish North American empire.

Someone should make a movie. . .

The Padre of Padre Island

ONE OF TEXAS' MOST UNIQUE PHYSICAL FEATURES is Padre Island, a 130 mile long sand barrier that extends along the coast of South Texas. It is the longest and largest barrier island in the United States, and comprises a total of 133,918 acres, although in no place is the island wider than three miles. It serves as natural protection from sea storms, and is a prized resort development at its north and south ends, while its central portion has been preserved as a protected National Seashore. The island was first depicted as "Isla Blanca" on a crude map drawn during the Alonzo Álvarez de Pineda expedition in 1519, and over the next approximately 300 years was known by various names, but the one that "stuck" was Isla del Padre Ballí, named after José Nicolás Ballí, a Franciscan Friar who inherited the initial land grant on the island, and became the first to improve and establish a stock raising operation there. Eventually, the name was shortened to just "Padre Island."

Ballí was born in Reynosa in 1770. His family was prominent in the area, and he and his brothers continued that tradition. Brothers Juan José and José María pursued military careers and served as officers in both the Tamaulipas militia and the Frontier Cavalry. José Nicolás decided on a different path and became a Catholic priest. He attended seminary in Monterrey and was ordained in 1791. He lived first in Matamoros, and then later in Refugio, but he conducted services all over the vast expanses of the Rio Grande Valley. He became the secular priest at the Refugio mission in 1804 and served in that capacity until his death in 1829. He oversaw the construction of the "new" Church of Nuestra Señora de Refugio, and was also listed as the treasurer and tithe collector for all the churches on the Rio Grande.

He owned extensive properties in South Texas, most inherited from relatives, and almost all of them operated as profitable stock operations. Those properties included what was officially known as the "Isla de Santiago" grant, which was what would become Padre Island. King Charles II had granted the island to Ballí's grandfather—also named Nicolás in 1759—but it had remained unimproved and unused since then. Padre Ballí requested a clear title to the property in 1827, with the intention of establishing additional grazing land for his herds in South Texas.

Padre Ballí had the island surveyed, and also granted colonization rights to families to live on the land, most of whom would work for him tending his herds. Naturally, he built a church, both for the conversion of the few Karankawa left in the area and for the island's residents. He based his operation on the extreme southern tip of the island and called it El Rancho Santa Cruz de Buena Vista. His primary stock was cattle, but he also raised horses and was well known for having the most hardy stock of mules in all of South Texas. Ballí left the day-to-day supervision of the island ranch to his nephew Juan José Ballí, who lived on the island.

Padre Ballí did not live long enough to see the full flowering of his stock operation on the island named for him. He died in Matamoros in April 1829. The final decree of granting the clear title to him did not officially come through until December 1829. The priest's will had granted half the island to Juan José, with the rest divided among other relatives. Juan José remained and operated the ranch until his death in 1853, and by that time the island had become known by its present moniker. Surprisingly, even after Texas' independence in 1836, Padre Island remained a possession of Mexico until the Treaty of Guadalupe Hidalgo ended the U.S.-Mexican War. Texas then approved the title of the Ballí family, but only after legal wrangling that left the family seriously cash poor, which hindered their operations. They also had to deal with squatters, such as the John Singer family, who built a house and began to live there after they were shipwrecked in 1847. Singer would also establish a ranch, and most likely "appropriated" his stock from some of the wandering Ballí herds. After Juan Jose's death in 1853, the family lost control of their lands, and it would pass through several hands before it reached its present status. The Ballí family has never received any compensation for the seizure of their family lands, despite a number of attempts through the courts. However, the legacy of Padre Ballí does live on—somewhat—in the name.

Texas Renaissance Man: Jose Antonio Navarro

TEXAS HAS CERTAINLY HAD ITS SHARE of people of many talents—politicians, military leaders, men and women of letters, among others—citizens who seemed to be the ones who excelled and led whenever the times called for it. Most of these gifted individuals seemed to have a specialty, a "field" in which they shined, but some found success in multiple arenas at multiple times. One of these was Jose Antonio Navarro, a man from a noble family with a frontier education who became one of Texas' true "renaissance men."

Born in San Antonio in 1795 to Angel Navarro—a native of Corsica—and Josefa Maria Ruiz y Pena, whose family came from the Spanish aristocracy, Jose Antonio Navarro was destined to be a leader from his beginnings. His family was one of the most important in San Antonio, and he would certainly follow in their footsteps. Like many Tejano families in San Antonio, the Navarro's supported the fledgling Mexican independence movement that began in 1810, which led young Jose—although he was just barely eighteen—to become involved with the ill-fated Gutierrez-Magee expedition in 1813. That experience as a revolutionary forced him to flee to the United States for a few years, and upon his return he read for the law and began to build one of the most prestigious practices in San Antonio. He would marry Margarita de la Garza in 1825 and it looked as if he would settle into the life of a Bexar patrician, but Jose Navarro was still a "revolutionary" at heart.

Navarro met and friended Stephen F. Austin in the 1820s. The two men were approximately the same age, both lawyers, and when they met, both bachelors. With so much in common it was natural that they would become close friends. Navarro taught Austin much about Mexican politics and culture, and Austin instilled in Navarro a passion for helping to colonize and populate Texas. Navarro the Mexican attorney used his knowledge of Mexican land law, as well as his political connections, to help a number of *empresario's* gain land contracts, and he eventually became the land commissioner for Green Dewitt's colony, which was adjacent to Austin's near the Lavaca River. His work led him to begin to passionately believe that Texas should be a separate state in the Mexican republic. He also became a committed Mexican Federalist.

Navarro began a career in politics in the 1830s when he was elected first to the *Coahuila y Tejas* state legislature, and then to the Mexican Congress. In both capacities he became a strong supporter of land grants and liberal colonization for Texas. Navarro was a Federalist, and as such first supported President Santa Anna when he came to office in 1833, but like almost all other Federalists broke with him when the President declared himself a Centralist in 1834. When Santa Anna dissolved the Mexican states, Navarro decided to cast his lot with the mostly American Texians in their dispute with Santa Anna. But, this Mexican patriot was not yet ready to disavow his national allegiance, and his support was limited to making Texas a separate state and a return of the Mexican federation. However, when it became apparent that Santa Anna was determined to crush all opposition to his rule, Navarro accepted Texas independence and became one of the original signers of the Texas Declaration of Independence at Washington-on-the-Brazos on March 2, 1836.

After independence Navarro continued his political activity when he became a Congressmen from Bexar County. He also became a supporter of Mirabeau B. Lamar, which meant he opposed Sam Houston, but his most strident support came in defense of Tejano land and citizenship rights, civil liberties that had come under constant attack from Anglos within Texas after independence. Perhaps thinking that expansion would help such a cause, or maybe out of political loyalty, Navarro accepted a role in the disastrous Santa Fe Expedition in 1841. When Mexican troops captured the Texian soldiers in New Mexico, the Mexican authorities gave him the opportunity to repudiate the Texas Republic and his fellow soldiers. Navarro defiantly refused and took his place among the prisoners taken back to Veracruz. The Mexican authorities condemned him to death and held him in prison for more than a year, but sympathetic Mexican army officials eventually helped him escape back to Texas.

Back in Texas he resumed his political activities, and he became a staunch advocate for Texas' annexation to the United States. When Texas became a part of the U.S. Navarro became an instrumental part of drafting the first state constitution, and he also would serve three terms in the Texas Senate, where he once again advocated for the rights of Tejanos. He retired from politics in 1849 to live the life of a gentleman rancher on his ranch near San Geronimo Creek east of San Antonio near Seguin.

Jose Antonio Navarro, however, was not a man to be idle. He began to chronicle his life and the events that surrounded it, writing historical and political essays for the *San Antonio Ledger*. Navarro freely advocated his positions on freedom and democracy, exalting the concept of American freedom and democracy, while also taking Texas' leaders to task for forgetting the contributions and rights of Tejanos. He also wrote very fine histories of the Texas independence movement and the Mexican War. His health began to fail in the 1860s, so he sold his ranch and moved back to San Antonio, where he died in 1871. The local newspaper probably summed up the gratitude and prominence that Texas felt for Navarro when in his obituary appeared this line: "To none of her greatest statesmen nor to her many eminent patriots is Texas more indebted for her existence than to Jose Antonio Navarro."

Texas' Soldier: Albert Sidney Johnston

WHEN ONE VISITS THE TEXAS STATE CEMETERY in Austin one of the first things that catches the eye is a wonderful stone monument contained within a white wrought iron fence at the center of the burial ground. It depicts a distinguished looking man in repose, the resting place of a person of obvious prominence. As one draws nearer to the plot the inscription reads that the grave contains the remains of Albert Sidney Johnston, a man who served as an officer in three armies during his lifetime: The United States of America, The Republic of Texas, and The Confederate States of America.

Born in Kentucky in 1803, Johnston grew up as the son of a fairly well-to-do farming family. At the age of eighteen he entered Transylvania University for a short time before receiving an appointment to the United States Military Academy in 1822. After graduating from West Point, the army posted him first in New York and then, in 1827, as an officer with the Sixth Infantry, in Missouri. He married a general's daughter, the former Henrietta Preston in 1829, and she and Albert prepared to make a soldier's life in Missouri.

The Johnston's welcomed a son and two daughters to their growing family, but Henrietta Johnston's health began to deteriorate after the birth of their last daughter. Because an officer's life can be one of many relocations, something that his wife's condition could hardly stand, Johnston took the difficult step of resigning his commission in 1834. He settled into the life of a farmer near St. Louis. Henrietta Johnston died in August 1835. Distraught, Johnston entrusted his children to his wife's family and did what many rootless men did in 1836—he went to Texas to fight in the Texas Revolution.

When he arrived in Texas the former United States army officer and graduate of West Point immediately enlisted in the Texas Army—as a private. Johnston arrived too late to see any action in the war, but the army's commander-in-chief, Thomas J. Rusk, recognized Johnston's experience and training and named him an adjunct general. President Sam Houston tapped him to be the brigadier general in command of the army in 1837. The appointment, like so much else in those days of the Republic, was mired in political factionalism and turmoil. President Houston was of the opinion that the previous general, Felix Huston, had used the army not for the good of the Republic but for personal gain and profit. Huston, naturally, saw it differently and in an attempt to restore his honor challenged the new commander—Johnston—to a duel. Huston seriously wounded Johnston, an injury that forced him into a long convalescence and unable to assume his command.

After his recovery in 1839, new Texas president Mirabeau Lamar made Johnston his secretary of war, and then sent him to help lead the expulsion of the Cherokee from East Texas. He then returned to Kentucky in 1840 and married for the second time to Eliza Griffin, Henrietta's cousin. He and his new bride came back to Texas in 1843 and settled to a comfortable life on a plantation in Brazoria County.

Johnston once again returned to the battlefield in 1846 during the Mexican War as a colonel of the First Texas Rifle Volunteers. He found that military life suited him, so he once again became a commissioned officer in the United States army. He served with distinction and honor on the Texas frontier, as part of the army escort of the Mormons to Salt Lake City, and finally with the Pacific Department in San Francisco in 1860.

Like so many officers from the South, Johnston faced a decision when secession became a reality in 1861, and like so many others Johnston proved to have more loyalty to state than country. He resigned his U.S. army commission for the second time in his life and returned to Texas. Confederate President Jefferson Davis then appointed the experienced Johnston to be his commander of the Western Department. He recruited an army of mostly Kentuckians and Tennesseans, and prepared to stop the Union invasion of the west.

Johnston's Confederate army was small, lacked any sort of military organization, and unlike the more celebrated Army of Northern Virginia, had to defend a very large swath of territory. Johnston relentlessly drilled his troops and did a good job of shoring up the region's defenses, although he was forced to relocate to Nashville and then to southern Tennessee. The Union army, under Ulysses S. Grant, began to move through Tennessee during the winter and early spring of 1862. Ultimately, Johnston would have to make a concentrated stand if he hoped to stop the U.S. invasion.

Johnston's Confederate troops met Grant's forces at the decisive Battle of Shiloh in April 1862. At the time it was fought it would be the bloodiest and costliest American battle of all time. Three days of fighting at Shiloh inflicted more American casualties than all the other wars, military excursions, or any martial actions had before it *combined*. One of those casualties was Albert Sidney Johnston. Shot through the leg on the first day of fighting, Johnston bled to death within hours. Deprived of his leadership, the Rebel forces eventually lost to Grant's troops at Shiloh, which ultimately paved the way to losing the Confederate west.

Upon his death Johnston was first interred in New Orleans, but after the war, in 1867, Texas brought its hero home and buried him in the plot that would become the Texas State Cemetery in Austin. His initial simple marker became the elaborate one of today in 1905 when the legislature commissioned sculptor Elizabeth Ney to fashion a more consequential monument to "Texas' soldier."

The Most Hated Man in Texas

PERHAPS THE MOST PERVASIVE OBJECT OF TEXAN derision is toward what we often not-so-affectionately call "Yankees." The evolution and etymology of that word and its full meaning would take much more room than this column allows, but in a general sense Texans use it to describe two kinds of people: folks who were born somewhere north of Oklahoma (we save a special sort of ridicule for those born in that state), and the soldiers and supporters of the Union during and after the Civil War. One would think that the extreme brand of hatred for "Yankees" came with the fighting of the Civil War, and some of the antipathy certainly did, but Texans saved their greatest ire toward "Yankees" for those who dominated the Radical Republican government in the state during Reconstruction. And the man who Texans hated the most during that trying period, Edmund J. Davis, was not by the strictest definition a "Yankee.' Instead, he was a native-born Floridian who had made Texas his adopted home years before that terrible war began.

Born in San Augustine, Florida in 1827, Davis made his way to Galveston to try his hand as a lawyer in 1848. He left Galveston in 1849 and moved to Laredo, where he became a customs official. From there, in 1853, he went to Brownsville and would eventually become the Twelfth District Judge. From his seat as a judge, Davis opposed the secession movement that had developed in the state in the years before the Civil War, and became a fervent supporter of Sam Houston, who shared Davis' views on secession. The majority of Texans did not share Davis and Houston's resistance to withdrawal from the Union, and in February 1861 the state did secede and join the Confederate States of

America. Edmund J. Davis, like Houston, refused to take a Confederate loyalty oath and thus the state removed him from office.

Sam Houston retired to his home in Huntsville after his removal from office; Edmund J. Davis took a different path when he recruited a cavalry regiment in South Texas and became a colonel in the Union army. After the war, Davis became a very active member of the Radical Republicans, the branch of that party that favored punishment and a strident program for re-entry toward the former states. He became a delegate from South Texas to the Constitutional Convention of 1868, a body that elected him president in 1869. As the head of the convention, it would be Davis who would press a program that disenfranchised those who supported secession, greatly expanded African American rights, and advocated a more powerful role for the state government.

The passage of the constitution of 1869 meant that Texas had to elect a new governor, and Davis ran against another, more conservative Republican (most Democrats were ineligible for office), Andrew Jackson Hamilton. Davis won a fairly comfortable victory and immediately began instituting a Radical Republican agenda within the state. Davis and the Republican dominated legislature formed the State Police Force and State Militia, which would include many former slaves as its members, to help combat the extreme lawlessness that had plagued the state since the end of the war. The state took greater control of and increased funding for public schools, began a series of infrastructure improvements, and the governor gained greater control over the power of appointments. In short, state power grew to unprecedented heights and Davis became the most powerful governor in the state's history.

He may have been powerful, but he was not popular. Republicans on the whole never had a chance of becoming a force in Texas politics as Reconstruction progressed and more former Confederates regained voting and citizenship rights. The Radical wing of the party was even more marginal, and the majority of Texans vehemently opposed their policy of increasing state power and expanding rights to African Americans. As the symbol of Radical power, revulsion toward Davis increased and Democrats targeted him for defeat in the election of 1873.

Davis never had a chance. Democrat Richard Coke soundly defeated him in December 1873, and Texans did not even want to wait until his constitutional term ended in March 1874 to remove him from office. The legislature, with Coke's acquiescence, forced Davis from office in January 1874. After his term, Davis remained a leader of Texas Republicans, and even ran for governor again in 1880, but he died generally forgotten in Austin in 1883.

When the Democrats regained control of the state's politics and the governor's chair they would remain in power for more than a century. Although it is hard to believe, Texas would not elect another Republican as governor for over one hundred years when Bill Clements defeated John Hill in 1978. If you visit the State Cemetery in Austin a tall, obelisk monument will catch your eye. Surely it is a commemoration to someone Texans greatly revere. As you move closer you will discover that it belongs to Edmund Jackson Davis, a man who during his lifetime was once the "most hated man in Texas."

Doing the Best That He Could Under Trying Conditions: Norris Wright Cuney

HISTORIAN JAMES SMALLWOOD CALLED the Reconstruction and the immediate aftermath a "time of hope and a time of despair" for African Texans. The end of slavery and the initial period under Republican rule provided a glimmer of hope for the Freedmen, but the return of Democratic rule under the "redeemers" snatched that hope away and brought about a period of violence, intimidation, and eventually Jim Crow—the despair to which Smallwood refers. And it was a time of long odds and struggle, but it was also a time that witnessed success against long odds and the formation of a community that developed a viable life, kept family ties whole, and also bred leaders who would keep hope alive for future generations.

One of those leaders was Norris Wright Cuney, a politician, labor organizer, party activist, and civil rights pioneer. Cuney was born in May, 1846 near Hempstead, the son of his white owner, Phillip Cuney, and slave mother, Adeline Stuart. His mixed parentage led his father to intervene and send Norris to George B. Vashon's Wylie Street School for Blacks in Pittsburgh, Pennsylvania in 1859; he remained at the school until the beginning of the Civil War. The fallout and turmoil after the end of the Civil War sent Cuney on a "wandering" period in which he frequented riverboats and worked at odd jobs primarily on wharves and docks in Texas. He eventually married in 1871 and settled in Galveston, where he studied law and became the president of the Galveston Union League.

Once established in Galveston, Cuney became prominent within the nascent Republican Party in Texas. He was a key supporter and organizer among former slaves for Governor Edmund J. Davis, who rewarded Cuney by making him the secretary of the Republican State Executive Committee. He ran for a number of elective offices during the late 1870s and 1880s, including mayor of Galveston and state representative, but lost each election. His losses, however, did not diminish his stature in the Republican Party, a position that allowed him to dispense patronage from the federal Republican government through the 1880s. He further entrenched his power with his appointment as the customs inspector and the customs collector at the port of Galveston. He would eventually become an alderman on the Galveston City Council and the national committeeman from Texas for the Republican Party. The latter position made him the most prominent southern African American in national politics.

Cuney next began to parley his political power into personal opportunity, as well as attempting to aid other African Americans in Galveston and Texas. He organized the black dockworkers in the city in 1883, and from his personal funds established the Screwmen's Benevolent Association to help African American stevedores compete for jobs and concessions on Galveston's docks and within its dominant shipping industry. From this position, Cuney became a powerful figure in Galveston's burgeoning union movement and the leading proponent of the city's African American community.

Cuney realized the advantages his education had given him, so he also worked diligently at promoting the cause of African American education. He became the school director of Galveston County in 1871, and for years made sure that the city's segregated schools received some semblance of adequate funding. He was also an early advocate and a key supporter of the first state supported black college in Texas at Prairie View.

Norris Wright Cuney was not without his critics. Naturally, many white Texans viewed him unfavorably and worked to limit his power, but neither did all African Texans support Cuney's activities and tactics. Cuney was not directly combative; he quite often advocated working within the system to effect change. Some accused him of "cronyism" in awarding patronage and in his business and political dealings. In some sense perhaps such criticisms had merit, but those who made them probably did not understand the context and tenor of the times. Cuney lived in a world of white superiority, a system that was intentionally constructed to limit any African American advancement. If he hoped to transform and better any segment of Texas' society he had to do so without grossly offending the hegemonic white establishment. Until his death in 1898, Norris Wright Cuney did the best he could under trying conditions, a man who lived precariously suspended between two worlds and two societies, just doing whatever he could to make one world advance and the other accept humane conditions for its oppressed members. For that, he deserves recognition.

Waco's Baritone Maestro: Jules Bledsoe

THERE MAY BE NOTHING AS PLEASING TO THE EAR as a well-trained baritone singing an operatic classic as it is intended to be sung. A deep timbre vocalizing the strains of a classically lyrical piece is enough to give anyone chills of joy. What many may not know is that one of the best and most famous American baritones of the early twentieth century was Waco's Jules Bledsoe, who was one of the first African American opera greats.

Julius Lorenzo Cobb Bledsoe was born in Waco in 1897. His father Henry L. Bledsoe was the pastor of the New Hope Baptist Church (his grandfather, Stephen Cobb, founded the church shortly after the Civil War) in that city, and Jules—as his parents called him—acquired his love of spirituals and religious messages from him. But, by all accounts, he gained his musical talent from his mother Jessie Cobb Bledsoe, who was a talented musician and singer in her own right, who encouraged young Jules to develop his talent. Bledsoe's parents divorced when he was only two, and he lived with his mother and his grandparents, but he kept contact with his father and was a vital member of New Hope throughout his youth. He sang his first concert—and he did it as a solo—at the church when he was but five years old.

Jules Bledsoe enrolled at Central Texas Academy when he was 8, and remained there until he graduated in 1905. Bledsoe, of course, excelled in music, but he was also an outstanding academic student. He first got a degree from Bishop College in Marshall in 1918, left the state for Virginia Union for post-grad studies, and then he enrolled at Columbia University, where he studied medicine from 1920-1924. But Bledsoe was not destined to be a physician; his true passion remained music, and during all his studies he also worked on his voice with Claude Waford, Luigi Parisotti, and Lazar Samiloff. In the end, it would be his voice that would bring him fame.

He made his professional debut in New York's Aeolian Hall on Easter Sunday 1924. He performed a program that included Handel, Bach, and Brahm's and when he was done the audience gave him a rousing ovation. Bledsoe had learned to sing in multiple languages, a talent much in demand for opera performers. Over the next three years he apprenticed with a number of opera companies, and performed as a bit performer in a few shows, but in 1927 he had a breakout role when he portrayed Joe in a production of Oscar Hammerstein II's *Showboat*. As Joe, he performs the classic song "Ol' Man River," and it was his version that became the standard and one that has been heard by millions throughout the world. Bledsoe said in an interview in the 1930s the he guessed he had sung the lyric "tote that barge/lift that bale" more than 20,000 times.

After *Showboat*, Bledsoe was in demand. His ability to sing in several languages (besides English he sang in French, Italian, and Spanish), along with possessing one of the smoothest, most clear, and deeply touching timbres in the world, made him one of the most sought after performers. He sang with symphonies, orchestras, lyric theaters, and, of course, opera companies. It was in opera that he found his greatest fame. He performed as Amonsaro in Verdi's *Aida*, as the title character in Mussorgsky's *Boris Godunov*. He didn't limit his experience to just operas, as he also appeared in motion pictures such as *Old Man Trouble*, *On the Levee*, and *Dear Old Southland*, as well as *Santa Fe Trail* (although he was uncredited in that movie because the producers did not want to give an African American too much credit and fame). Unfortunately, in those films, Bledsoe—a well-educated and erudite man—was forced to play the role of the stereotypical "Jim Crow" era black man, one of low intelligence and an almost childlike mien.

Bledsoe also had a recording career. Besides recording traditional baritone solos in the manner of a traditional oratorio, he returned to his "roots" quite often with albums of traditional spirituals. He made "Ol' Man River" the most recognizable version of that song;

his recording of "Swing Low, Sweet Chariot," also became the most widely heard standard. Odds are that you have heard his version, sung in a deep bass, slowly and reverently.

Jules Bledsoe's career came to an abrupt end while he was still enjoying his fame. He was enjoying an evening with friends at the home of his longtime companion and theatrical agent Freddye Huygens in Hollywood after he had appeared at a War Bond Drive. As he sat and visited with his gathered friends he suddenly slumped over dead of a massive and sudden cerebral hemorrhage. He was but forty-five. Huygens made sure he was returned to his hometown of Waco for burial, where he is interred in that city's Greenwood Cemetery. Baylor University's Texas Collection houses Bledsoe's papers and sheet music, along with other material culture.

A Women's Rights Pioneer

2019 IS UPON US AND IT IS AMAZING TO THINK that in just one year it will be the centennial anniversary of women's right to vote in the United States. It was not until the 19th Amendment to the Constitution went into effect in 1920 that females received universal suffrage. Again, think about that for a moment—less than one hundred years ago. Incredible, isn't it?

East Texas can claim one of its own as a leader of the movement to gain votes for women. Minnie Fisher Cunningham, a native of New Waverly in Walker County, became perhaps the most visible, vocal, and vociferous leader for women's suffrage in the state. Born on family land near New Waverly in 1882, Cunningham accomplished much during her eighty-two year life; she was one of the first Texas women to receive a pharmacy degree, ran for U.S. Senator in 1928, worked for the Agricultural Adjustment Administration during the New Deal, and campaigned for the governor's mansion in 1944. But it was her work for women's voting rights that brought her the most notoriety.

After receiving her pharmacy degree from the University of Texas Medical Branch at Galveston in 1901, Cunningham worked as a pharmacist in Huntsville for a year, but she became incensed at the inequality she encountered. It seems that the newly hired male pharmacists, some who did not have near the education she had, received more money in their pay envelopes at the end of the week. "It made a suffragette out of me," she told a biographer late in her life, so she left her job, married reform-minded lawyer Beverly Cunningham, and embarked on a campaign to give Texas' women equal rights under the law.

After she and her husband relocated to Galveston in 1907, Cunningham became a leader in the island city's suffrage movement. She served as president of the Galveston Equal Suffrage Association and began to tour the state to gain support for the cause. In 1915 she began the first of four terms as president of the Texas Equal Suffrage Association (TESA), and became directly responsible for fantastically increasing the number of Association Chapters in the state. During four terms as president (1915-1919), she built TESA to a membership of more than 10,000, and established a ground organization in every senatorial district in the state.

Cunningham was generally unhappy in her marriage, largely due to Beverly's incessant alcoholism and his frustration with her political activity. The marriage became further strained when Minnie moved to Austin in 1917 to open the state suffrage headquarters. James Ferguson, Texas' governor during the earliest part of Cunningham's organization presidency, opposed votes for women and he worked to keep the issue away from the state's voters. However, when the legislature removed Ferguson from office for financial malfeasance, the new office-holder, William P. Hobby of Houston, took an interest in the issue and helped bring the issue to Texas' voters. Cunningham lobbied Hobby on the issue, and was directly involved in negotiation efforts that led the Texas legislature to pass legislation that allowed the state's women to vote in the 1918 primary elections. For the first time in the state's history, women played a role in selecting the leaders of the state, and became a key constituency of Governor Hobby. Surprisingly, however, a referendum that would have allowed women to vote in the state's general election failed, which is one reason why Minnie Fisher Cunningham decided that she needed to take her voice to a national stage.

Cunningham shifted her focus to securing a Constitutional Amendment that would give women the universal franchise in the United States. She traveled to Washington D.C. and lobbied congressmen and other leaders, and played a large role in the eventual passage of the 19th Amendment. Since states now had to approve the new Amendment, Cunningham began to travel to individual states, shilling for suffrage and using her unique persuasive qualities. Finally, the 19th Amendment became law and women became eligible to vote for the first time in 1920. Cunningham would go on to help organize the National League of Women's Voters in 1920, and became one of four Texas women elected as a delegate-at-large to the Democratic National Convention. She became the leading advocate for the nation's first social welfare law, the Maternity and Infancy Act, which became law in 1921. It provided federal funds to establish prenatal care facilities, mostly in rural states.

Cunningham returned to Texas in 1928 and ran for the senate, but she finished far back in the primary. Her husband also died during the campaign, although the two had been separated for more than a decade. Cunningham worked as an editor for the Texas A&M University Agricultural Extension Service from 1930 to 1939, and in that role became a tireless advocate for New Deal anti-poverty programs. She returned to Washington in 1939 to work for the Agricultural Adjustment Agency. When she returned to Texas in 1944 she joined with other Texas New Dealers to begin to oppose Governor Coke Stevenson and his "Texas Regular" campaign. She toured the state speaking against the anti-FDR initiative, and was a key factor in Texas voters rejecting the movement. She continued to work for liberal causes well into her seventies, and when she died in December 1964, she had just been the Walker County campaign chief for Lyndon Johnson's successful presidential campaign.

So, about one hundred years ago a diminutive but forceful East Texas woman made it her life's work to make sure the United States finally lived up to its promise of political equality no matter your gender. Less than one hundred years—that is not that long past, is it?

The First Country Star: Vernon Dalhart

TAKE A FEW SECONDS AND INDULGE ME in an exercise. Picture in your mind a country music star, a soulful crooner of the "common man." What image appeared in your head? Was it someone with a cowboy hat, jeans, and a western yoked shirt? Perhaps it was one of the younger singers around today, someone who dresses very informally, to say the least. I am certain that you did not picture someone in a top hat and tails—that is just not "country." I am also very sure that you did not "hear" anyone who sang in operas. Our images are singed into our minds and they very often cannot be moved, but surprisingly the "first" country star—Vernon Dalhart—did not fit our stereotype. Instead, he was an opera singer first and always appeared on stage in his elegant attire.

The man who would become the first acknowledged country singer's parents did not christen him Vernon Dalhart. He was born Marion Try Slaughter II, after his grandfather, in Jefferson, TX in 1883. His family name also did not have the most sterling of reputations in the East Texas river town. His namesake was a troublesome bully who regularly picked fights in Jefferson taverns, and was also a leading member of the county's incarnation of the Ku Klux Klan. Robert Slaughter, Slaughter II's father, did not fall far from the family tree. While he was ostensibly a rancher, he spent much of his time drinking, fighting, and carousing. His peccadilloes would eventually lead to the most traumatic incident in his son's life when Bob Castleberry, his mother's brother who always believed that his sister had married far below her station, shot and killed Robert Slaughter. The town obviously agreed with the Castleberry side of the family as they refused to indict and jail Uncle Bob.

After his father's death, Try (as they called him) and his mother moved to Dallas. The larger city gave Try access to a formal education in music and he excelled. He began to sing in productions and in other venues around Dallas, as well as also occasionally "cowboying" to support the family. He got married in 1902 and very quickly fathered two children. His mother remarried in 1905 and relieved of the burden of caring for her he moved his young family to New York to study opera. He was cast in some bit parts, including one in Puccini's *The Girl of the Golden West*, but it was a struggle to make ends meet.

Finally, he got a break. After the pain of being a minor player in the Puccini opera, he was picked to be a principal player. He had finally made the program, but he needed a name so he chose for a moniker two West Texas towns where he had once worked as a cowboy. Thus he became "Vernon Dalhart," and he also became at least a minor operatic star. He toured with his company throughout the U.S. and Canada, and then began to gain roles with other operatic touring companies, where he sang in French and Italian as well as English. He became a bona fide star in 1914 when he took on the role of Ralph Rackstraw in a production of the now Gilbert and Sullivan classic *H.M.S. Pinafore*. The critics praised his performance and it opened the door for him to take on other roles, although he would never again scale the heights of opera fame that he did in *Pinafore*.

Of course, it was another musical genre in which Dalhart gained his immortal fame. Dalhart began to record for Edison and Columbia records in the 1910s and early 1920s, soundtracks that had some moderate success, and he sang in all sorts of styles. The change came in 1924. Dalhart heard a recording of *The Wreck of the Southern Old 97* and he convinced Edison executives to let him record it. Records in those days needed a "flip side," so Dalhart also recorded a song that most agree was written by his cousin titled *The Prisoner's Song*. The big difference was that he arranged and sang it as a folk song in his naturally twangy Texas accent, which he usually took great pains to hide.

As often happens, it was the "B" side that became a hit, and the public clamored for more Dalhart songs in the style of *Prisoner*. Never one to disappoint his public, he obliged and by 1925 Vernon Dalhart, with guitarist Carson Robbins as an accompanist, began exclusively singing what were now being called "country" songs. Dalhart had been the major player in creating a new genre. Soon, Jimmie Rodgers eclipsed even Dalhart in popularity, and the Carter Family combined their gospel roots with the new music to also become a huge act. Vernon Dalhart made a fortune and built a mansion in the New York countryside.

Then the Great Depression changed everything. Dalhart, heavily invested in the stock market, lost much of his fortune. Other country stars made the bulk of their money at personal appearances and traveling the nation, but Dalhart had never toured. When he finally did country fans were not sure what to make of this man who appeared on stage in a tuxedo looking as if he were about to sing in an opera. His concert career never took off, and his record sales suffered.

His career in shambles, Dalhart tried his hand at a number of occupations through the 1940s, including teaching voice and working as a security guard. His health also began to suffer as years of privation began to take its toll. He was working as a bell man at a Bridgeport, CT hotel in January 1948 when he had a heart attack. He never fully recovered and a second attack took his life in September of that year, the end of the line for the man who is credited with being the "first" country singer.

From Mess Attendant to Hero: Doris Miller and Pearl Harbor

I HAVE A CONFESSION TO MAKE. Like many historians I often get wrapped up in other things that I forget the significance of, even the approach, of significant dates. So, when my friend Malcolm Rector once asked me if I was planning to write on Pearl Harbor I had to admit that I had fully forgotten that December 7 was drawing near. Thanks to Malcolm I "remembered."

The Japanese attack on Pearl Harbor caught the nation flat-flooted, and also led us into World War II. Servicemen and women from all over the United States became heroes that dreadful day as they courageously dealt with an assault that was not only a surprise but particularly brutal. One man, Texan Doris Miller, became an unlikely hero through an act of bravery that is still celebrated when he became the first African American hero of World War II.

Born and raised in Willow Grove in 1919, Doris Miller attended high school in Waco. After graduation Miller worked a few odd jobs around Waco, but just a month before he turned twenty in 1939, Doris Miller enlisted in the United States Navy. Miller entered the Navy as a Mess Attendant, third class. The nation's military, like American society of the era, was a segregated and discriminatory institution. The U.S. Navy may have been the most racially offensive of all the branches. The Navy recruited African Americans only to the Steward's Branch at that time, sailors whose sole job was to work in services galleys and laundries; they were excluded from any other service.

The Navy assigned Miller to the *U.S.S. West Virginia*, a battleship anchored in Pearl Harbor on December 7, 1941. While there have been a number of accounts of Miller's action on the day Franklin Roosevelt said would "live in infamy," the most authoritative have Miller performing laundry duties when the alarm for General Quarters sounded. As he made his way to his assigned battle station, Miller helped get mortally wounded Captain Mervyn Bennion—the *West Virgina's* commander—to a safer place than the ship's fiery deck, and then another officer instructed him to deliver ammunition to the machine guns on the deck. When Miller reached the guns he found them unmanned, so he began to fire at attacking Japanese Zeroes, operating a weapon on which he had never trained. When later asked how he did so, Miller replied, "It wasn't hard. I just pulled the trigger and she worked fine." Miller fired the weapon for at least twenty minutes before the flames on the deck forced him and his fellow seamen to leap into the ocean.

The story at this point becomes blurred and mired in controversy and the American obsession with race. Some may blame the proverbial "fog of war," and certainly Secretary of the Navy Frank Knox's news blackout in the days after the attack contributed to the lack of full accounts about Miller's heroics. The better explanation may be just plain racism. Whatever the reason, Miller's actions were not immediately acknowledged; the official account would eventually not even agree on how many aircraft Miller shot down. He insisted that he vanquished at least six airborne attackers, and other witnesses claimed he shot down four, but the official Navy account gave Miller credit for only one kill.

Worse were the official Navy releases about the incident. Secretary Knox's initial reports made a reference to a "seaman aboard a battleship" who ". . .blasted an attacking torpedo plane," but it never identified the "seaman." Later reports have credit on to "a Negro mess attendant," and also misidentified the ship as the doomed *U.S.S. Arizona*. While the Navy could not bother to identify the "Negro mess attendant," who was well known to his shipmates, they did begin to glorify the exploits of white sailors and aviators as heroes—men they identified by name. For three months the heroic soldier on the deck of the *West Virginia* went unnamed.

Finally, after pressure from civil rights groups and some politicians, in March 1942 the Navy gave Miller his due. Secretary Knox issued a standard letter of citation. But that was it—no more. By comparison, the Navy awarded the Navy Cross to a white sailor who rescued nine aviators on life rafts. Some newspaper outlets and the NAACP actively asked the Navy and President Roosevelt why Doris Miller received no similar honors. They had their effect. Secretary Knox announced in May that Doris Miller would receive the Navy Cross.

Miller had little time to reflect on his achievement. He was a sailor, and sailors go where they are sent. The Navy sent the Mess Attendant to the aircraft carrier *Liscome Bay*; unfortunately his heroics did not change the Navy's discriminatory practice of keeping African American sailors only in the Steward's Branch. The *Liscome Bay* sailed to the South Pacific, and during the Battle of the Gilbert Islands in November 1943 the ship took a torpedo and sank into the Pacific. Doris Miller, along with all 655 men he served with perished. He was 24. Today Doris Miller is hailed as a hero with a naval ship named in his honor as well as numerous places in his Waco home, a fitting tribute to a hero who fought and died so that the nation he loved might one day live up to the ideas it espoused. I think that he would be proud of the progress we have made.

Distinguished Defiance: Dr. Hector P. Garcia and Tejano Rights

I HAVE ALWAYS BEEN ATTRACTED TO THE stories of men and women who quietly, but steadfastly, stood up for what is right. Perhaps it is the dignity of such actions, or maybe I just like to see people who take a definitive stance, but whose actions suggest that it is the cause that is important not the self. That is why I have always had an affinity for the career of Dr. Hector P. Garcia and how he continually reminded Texas and America that both needed to do a better job of ending oppression for its citizens of Mexican descent, as well as honoring their contributions as Americans.

Garcia's roots stretched back to Spanish occupation of Mexico. His ancestors received a New World land grant directly from the King of Spain, and his family eventually made their way to Llera, Tamaulipas. The violence of the Mexican Revolution displaced many families in northern Mexico, and it caused the Garcias to flee their homeland in 1918 and move to Mercedes, TX when Hector was just seven years-old. The Garcia family operated a successful dry-goods business in Mercedes, and also sent six of their children off to college to obtain advanced degrees. Hector would graduate from the University of Texas, and then from the UT Medical School in Galveston in 1940.

Garcia was fresh from a two-year residency when he decided to serve his country and volunteer for the army in 1942 to fight in World War II. Despite his medical training, Garcia served first as an infantry officer and later as an engineer before eventually becoming a medical officer. During the war, Garcia earned six battle stars and a Bronze Star. His last posting was in Italy, where he met and married his wife Wanda Fusillo. Garica left the army in 1945 at the rank of major.

Garcia returned to Texas in 1946, probably with the intention of serving the people of Corpus Christi as a physician the rest of his life. He and his brother opened a small practice with the express purpose of serving anyone who needed care regardless of their ability to pay. Garcia also became active in the local LULAC Chapter, becoming its president in 1947. Such a position exposed Garcia to two injustices regularly applied to Mexican Americans in South Texas. One was that Mexican American veterans were regularly denied their full benefits, and the other was the intentional inadequacy of education for Mexican American children. During a bout with a deadly disease in 1947, Garcia overheard a school district employee brag about the city's segregation and "making sure the Mexicans are around to work." At that point, Garcia vowed to make sure he worked every day to end such oppression and attitudes.

After leaving the hospital, Garcia moved to establish an organization that would work to bring awareness to the plight of Tejanos and work to correct injustice. Because he had worked extensively with veterans, and also because he knew that the patriotism of former soldiers would not be questioned, Garcia made sure that the base of his new organization would be former members of the military. He called a meeting on March 26, 1948 to address the concerns of Tejano veterans, and from that meeting formed the American G.I. Forum. The Forum would soon establish chapters in more than forty Texas cities, and its activities would range from helping veterans obtain medical care, to ensuring education for migrant worker's children, to supporting LULAC activities to desegregate "Mexican Schools."

The American G.I. Forum, and its founder, gained even greater prominence through the Felix Longoria affair in 1949. Funeral home officials in Three Rivers, TX refused to re-inter Longoria's remains when they were returned from the Philippines. Why? Because the veterans section was in the "whites only" portion of the cemetery. Three Rivers officials rebuffed Garcia's initial efforts to have Longoria buried in his rightful section, so the G.I. Forum leader turned to newly elected senator

Lyndon Johnson to clear the way for Longoria to be placed in Arlington National Cemetery with full honors.

Garcia gained national recognition when he became the coordinator of the "Viva Kennedy-Viva Johnson" clubs during the 1960 presidential election. During the 1950s Garcia and the AGIF had avoided becoming associated with one party, and he had cultivated relations with Democrat and Republican alike, but with his role in the Kennedy campaign Garcia had clearly made a choice to cast his lot with the Democrats. Kennedy would disappoint Garcia when he failed to actually pursue a political agenda to aid Mexican Americans, but his relationship with fellow Texan Lyndon Johnson would prove more fruitful. Johnson would actively seek to improve the plight of Latinos, and he would also appoint Dr. Garcia to the United States Commission on Civil Rights.

Hector Garcia would continue to serve as a national presence throughout the 1970s, and he did so with quiet dignity. He pressed for improved conditions for *colonias* in South Texas, and greater political opportunities for all people of Hispanic descent. He did so while enduring great physical pain as he suffered from a number of medical maladies, from heart problems to stomach cancer. President Ronald Reagan awarded him the Presidential Medal of Freedom in 1984 in honor of his achievements, and in 1990 Pope John Paul II gave him the Order of St. Gregory the Great for his work on human rights, a fitting honor for a dignified man committed to ensuring that all people receive the entire promise of American liberty. Dr. Garcia died in 1996 of congestive heart failure.

Texas' Theater Auteur: Margo Jones

TEXAS HAS HAD NO SHORTAGE OF INNOVATIVE and celebrated playwrights, directors, actors, and choreographers. Texans such as Betty Buckley, Tommy Tune, Preston Jones, Mary Martin, Debbie Allen, and Terrance McNally have all made names for themselves on the stage. Margo Jones is another one of those icons that all who love the stage recognize. She was a pioneer of the American resident theater movement, and a producer and director of many of the nation's most famous playwrights and actors. In many ways Ms. Jones is responsible for the outstanding regional theatrical companies in Houston, Dallas, and other Texas and U.S. cities that served as a "training ground" for many of those listed above.

Born in Livingston in 1911, Margaret Virginia Jones' parents called her Margo from an early age. Jones was a vivacious and active child, who excelled in not only creative pursuits but in academic ones as well. After her high school graduation she attended what was then called the Girls' Industrial College of Texas, which is now Texas Women's University, in Denton. She left Denton with a BA in Speech and an MA in Psychology and Education, but her passion was for the theater.

She went to work at the Southwestern School of Theater in Dallas in the early 1930s. She would then move on to enroll at the Pasadena (CA) Playhouse Summer School so she could study directly with that entities influential founder and director Gilmor Brown. With such a credential in hand, Jones them traveled to Japan, China, England, and France before living for a while in New York, all places where she began to study and collect diverse information and techniques employed on stages throughout the globe. She had begun what would probably set her apart from many other stage producers and directors; she was as much a student and intellectual of the craft as she was an active participant.

Jones spent a short time as assistant director of the Houston Federal Theater Project, a New Deal initiative, and then founded the Houston Community Players in 1936, which she would direct for six years. She became a champion of the regional theater movement, and her active search for talent and dedication to developing new actors, writers, and directors led to great innovation and made Texas truly a breeding ground for the Broadway stage. Her dedication to an academic pursuit of the theater led her to next accept a position as an instructor at the University of Texas from 1942-1944. While there, through mutual acquaintances, she met Tennessee Williams, which led to a fruitful professional and personal relationship. She would direct a number of Williams' plays at regional playhouses such as Pasadena and Cleveland. Her deft direction gave Williams national notice, a key factor in his rise to prominence as perhaps the nation's best playwright.

Jones' regional productions led to what would become her most significant contribution to the American stage. New and promising authors, directors, and actors needed a setting to hone their craft, to become masters of their art before they embarked on a career on the nation's largest stages in New York. Communities and smaller cities also needed a way to see large-scale productions of heralded shows. Such a desire led Jones to seek to establish a network of nonprofit professional resident theaters outside of New York. Armed with a Rockefeller Foundation grant and the commercial success of directing Williams' *The Glass Menagerie*, Jones co-founded (with John Rosenfield, Jr.) the first of such entities in Dallas. Incorporated as the Dallas Civic Theatre, it opened in 1947 in the Gulf Oil Building in Fair Park. It was the first professional arena theater, and the first nonprofit resident one as well. Jones and the theater would through the years bring to Dallas classic productions of Shakespeare, Ibsen, and Chekhov, as well as contemporary plays by Williams, Dorothy Parker, and George Sessions Perry.

Jones continued to take plays to Broadway, but much of her focus became promoting and helping to establish resident theaters in other places. Jerome Lawrence and Robert E. Lee brought their play, *Inherit the Wind*, to Jones in 1955 after New York producers termed the play on the Scopes Trial as too controversial. Such did not concern Jones, and she staged the play to sold-out audiences in the Dallas in 1955, which gave the play the impetus to move on to Broadway and eventually a motion picture adaptation. Jones also gave many prominent actors such as Brenda Vaccaro, Larry Hagman, and Louis Latham their start by using them at the Dallas Civic Theater.

Margo Jones tragically died in July 1955 through accidental poisoning. A common chemical method used in the 1950s to clean carpets was carbon tetrachloride. It is highly effective, but also highly toxic if you breathe the fumes. After such a procedure, Jones came back to her apartment before the fumes had dispersed and collapsed and died before she could be helped. She no doubt had many contributions left to make to the world of the theater, but her vision, the nonprofit residential theaters, now produces the bulk of plays staged in the United States, and provides a vital "feeder" network for Broadway.

The Texan Member of the "Big Four:" James L. Farmer, Jr.

CHARISMATIC, FORCEFUL LEADERS HELPED to spur the modern, post World War II civil rights movement—often referred to as the "Second Reconstruction"—but many of their accomplishments have been overshadowed by the large persona that was Dr. Martin Luther King, Jr. King, without a doubt, deserves all the accolades that society has bestowed upon him, but he was not a lone leader. During that Second Reconstruction some often referred to the "Big Four" of the movement: King (Southern Christian Leadership Conference), Whitney Young (Urban League); Roy Wilkins (NAACP), and James L. Farmer, Jr., who was one of the principal founders of the Congress of Racial Equality (CORE), and who many commentators have hailed as the most successful direct action organizer of the era.

Born in Marshall, Texas, in 1920, Farmer's father was a professor at Wiley College. The elder Farmer was a racial pioneer in his own right; he was the first African American in Texas to hold a Ph.D., and helped to make Wiley College one of the most academically successful historically black colleges in the nation. Growing up in East Texas during the time of Jim Crow meant that the Farmer family had to continually deal with the tribulations of segregation. Although it would be hard to fathom today, Farmer had to often watch his father—a man whose education and intellect would have afforded him a certain degree of stature in almost any society other than the American South in the 1930s and 1940s—submit to and accept an inferior social standing due only to his race.

Farmer, Jr. was something of a child prodigy and he entered Wiley College at just fourteen. He came under the influence of Professor Melvin Tolson, an activist for the Southern Farmer's Tenant Union and a committed civil rights advocate. Tolson also coached the college's successful debate team, as depicted in the Denzel Washington film *The Great Debaters*, and the lessons Farmer learned while on that team proved invaluable to his later career.

After graduating from Wiley, Farmer moved on to Howard University School of Religion, where he received a Divinity degree in 1941. While at Howard another influential faculty member, Howard Thurman, introduced Farmer to the non-violent concepts of Mohandas Gandhi; like King, Farmer realized that such a philosophy was the best approach to subverting and exposing the brutality and inhumanity of segregation, discrimination, and racial oppression. He became involved in the Student League for Industrial Democracy—the forerunner of Students for a Democratic Society (SDS).

His activism led him to try to think of a new national organization that would combine the fight for civil rights with the larger fight for social justice of all oppressed peoples. After first trying to convince the Fellowship of Reconciliation (FOR) to expand and join his campaign, Farmer next moved to form a new group—the Congress of Racial Equality (CORE). Farmer's new organization would eventually lead some of the most important—and brutally suppressed—civil rights protests and actions in the nation. CORE members staged the famous sit-in at Greensboro, NC, and Farmer led dozens of marches and protests throughout the South. But the action CORE was most noted for were the "Freedom Rides."

Throughout the South, bus stations and depots were completely segregated; black riders were either forbidden from entering segregated bus facilities or were restricted to black-only waiting rooms, areas that were most often substandard and lacked basic necessities. Farmer and CORE organized the "Freedom Rides" to illuminate and protest such practices. Chartered integrated buses traveled from town to town in the South and peacefully tried to integrate the facilities. Southern racists, however, were not ready for such a change and the buses were most often met by mobs wielding sticks, torches, rocks, and other weapons. The Freedom Rides became one of the most powerful symbols of racial hatred during the era. Farmer had heard his whole life that there was no racial problem or oppression in the South, and that African Americans should be thankful they lived in such a free nation. Farmer knew better as he had lived with racial exclusion and subjugation since the day he was born. Although he was called a "traitor," and "un-American' for taking a stance, he persisted, and the U.S. and the nation became a better place because of his activism.

Farmer eventually became disenchanted with the changing face of the civil rights movement, particularly what he saw as a turn toward militancy and extremist sentiments associated with the Black Power movement. He resigned from CORE and returned to his first love, teaching, and accepted a position at Lincoln University in Missouri. He would unsuccessfully run for Congress in 1968 in New York as a candidate of the Liberal Party, which was a Republican backed organization. He lost that race to Democrat Shirley Chisholm, but Richard Nixon appointed him as the Assistant Secretary of the Department of Health, Education, and Welfare in 1969.

Farmer suffered from severe diabetes in his later years, but he remained active in pressing for equality and social justice. The Texan member of the "Big Four" died of diabetes complication in 1999, but he left behind a rich legacy of activism and the push for true equality in our nation.

She Stood Up For What Was Right: Lulu Belle White

PEOPLE OF COURAGE COME IN MANY SHAPES, sizes, religious preference, and races. If you ask people to picture courage in their mind most would think of an image of a soldier, a cowboy, or someone defending their home and hearth. Those are certainly profiles of courage, but there is also another kind of courage, one that may take more "guts" than physical actions—those people who defy conventional wisdom and fight and stand up for something that is not popular during their time. Such courage risks more than pain and bodily injury; it imperils one's social standing and endangers a reputation. In some cases that may be greater courage than facing down a foe intent on harm. Lulu Belle Madison White, a Texas civil rights activist in the 1940s and 1950s had such courage.

Born in Elmo to a rural farm family in 1907, Lulu Madison attended school in Elmo and Terrell before enrolling at Butler College in Tyler. She remained at Butler for only a year before she moved on to Prairie View A&M, where she received a BA in English in 1928. She then accepted a teaching position in a small school near Houston, where she met and married Julius White. After teaching for two years, White had a higher calling and left her job to take a full-time position with the Houston Chapter of the NAACP.

White believed that the advancement of African Texans was forever hindered by the presence of the "All-White Primary," which essentially eliminated black voices from the state's political decisions. Determined to make sure that Texas honored its obligation of voter equality, she devoted almost the entire decade of the 1930s to fighting the "All-White Primary" and other franchise barriers Texas placed before African Americans. Ultimately, with White's leadership and legal maneuvers by NAACP lawyers, the U.S. Supreme Court outlawed the insidiously discriminatory primary laws.

White found another campaign in 1937 when she became the organization's Director of Youth Council. She then became the Houston Chapter president and she, along with Juanita Craft of Dallas, became the primary chapter organizer and recruiter in Texas. Working closely with Craft, White established scores of NAACP chapters throughout Texas and the South, and she became one of the leading voices in the nation encouraging blacks to exercise their political rights. Under her tutelage, the Houston NAACP chapter became the largest and most well-funded in the South, and one of the most active in the nation. Lulu Belle White became the voice of African Texan voting rights, and she also became a target of white supremacists as she consistently received death threats and other attempts at intimidation.

She was not a women to back down, and as the 1940s moved toward the 1950s, White became the NAACP state director, and she also became actively involved in the campaign for educational equality. She worked tirelessly in the fight to integrate the University of Texas, and encouraged Heman Sweatt to bring his suit against the university. Sweatt credited her leadership as the ultimate key to success in the case, particularly when she, once again with Juanita Craft, helped to bring Thurgood Marshall to the state to argue the case that eventually forced UT to integrate its law school and professional programs.

Lulu White was still not finished. She next moved on to agitate for something very dear to her heart—the low and unequal pay for black public school educators. Pay in the 1950s for Texas teachers in white schools was low; the pay for the same job in the segregated African American schools was abysmally lower. She bombarded the state legislature with pleas to provide adequate pay for black teachers, and while she enjoyed only limited success her persistence did make a difference. Pay remained unequal, but black educators did begin to see a bit more in their pay envelopes.

Perhaps Lulu Belle Madison White frenetically moved to bring about change because she knew her time on earth was short. Still working at her post as state director, and still pressing for advancement, Lulu Belle White died of heart failure in July 1957. She was just fifty-years old, but she crammed a lifetime of achievement into those fifty years, and demonstrated every day what truly made her a courageous advocate for equal rights.

A Very Different and Reluctant Cold Warrior: Van Cliburn

TEXAS LOST A HERO IN 2013 WHEN VAN CLIBURN passed away in Fort Worth. Cliburn proved that heroes come in all shapes, sizes, and forms, for he was not a military, sports, or political star—the usual variety of Texas icons—but made his name as an internationally renowned classical pianist. The soft spoken, gentle Cliburn climbed from a life in the East Texas oil fields to the heights of musical stardom, and along the way, although he never asked or wished to be, became a symbol of the Cold War competition between the United States and the Soviet Union.

Harvey Levan Cliburn, Jr. was born in Shreveport, Louisiana in 1934 to a pianist mother, Rildia, and oil executive father, Harvey, Sr. Van, as his family called, began to play under his mother's instruction at age three and became quite the prodigy. His bloodlines certainly played some role; Rilidia Cliburn studied piano under Arthur Friedheim, who had studied under maestro Franz Liszt. Cliburn, however, showed promise above and beyond his genes. The family moved to Kilgore when Van was six, and at twelve he won his first statewide competition. At the same age, the budding star played with the Houston Symphony Orchestra, the youngest person to ever be allowed such an honor.

Cliburn enrolled at New York City's prestigious Julliard School when he was seventeen, where he came under the influence of Rosina Lhevinne. He began to focus his talents in the manner of the great Russian romantics, and became one of the most well-known Julliard students when he played at Carnegie Hall, among other venues throughout the city. There was no doubt that Van Cliburn was destined to be an American music star, but perhaps no one could have anticipated what heights the young Texan would climb.

The Cold War of the post-World War II years entangled the United States and the Soviet Union in an intense geopolitical conflict that spread across the globe. While the primary focus of the rivalry was within the political and military sphere, the enmity and competition between the two superpowers spilled over into the cultural realm as well. Athletic contests, such as the Olympics, became grudge matches between the competing philosophies, and the "space race" became a duel to see who could make the latest technological advances. The United States fared well in most of these clashes, but it seemed to lag behind the Soviets and their Russian tradition in some of the more "high-brow" cultural endeavors such as ballet and music. If an American could prevail in that arena it would become a notch in the belt for the U.S.

Van Cliburn would triumph in such a setting. The young pianist traveled to Moscow to participate in the first International Tchaikovsky Competition in 1958. To a large degree, the Soviets had designed the event to demonstrate Soviet cultural superiority over the U.S. and capitalism. It was essentially a Cold War propaganda tool, one that the Soviet communists hoped would capitalize upon their nation's other recent "victory," the launch of the Sputnik satellite. The competition did not go as the Soviets had planned. Russians understand exquisite classical piano, and as Cliburn finished playing "Tchaikovsky's Piano Concerto No. 1" and "Rachmaninoff's Piano Concerto No. 3" as a finale to the contest the Russian audience sprang to their feet and gave the young Texan an eight minute standing ovation. Despite the Soviet's best laid plans, it was Van Cliburn who emerged from Moscow the acknowledged winner.

Cliburn returned as a conquering hero. New York gave him a ticker-tape parade, *Time* magazine called him "The Texan Who Conquered Russia," and he traveled the country playing in concert halls before adoring audiences. He signed a lucrative record contract, and became the first classical pianist to have a platinum album. Most of all, President John F. Kennedy and other American politicians held him up as a symbol of the superiority of the American way of life. Cliburn, however, did not see himself as a hero of the Cold War. He always deflected any talk about rivalry, and maintained that any praise he received for his music was not indicative of the superiority of the United States but for that of classical music. In fact, he returned many times to play in the Soviet Union, and affection between him and his audience there was an anomaly during a time of almost vitriolic competition.

Humble as always, Van Cliburn chose to live in Fort Worth after his triumph rather than one of the "cultural centers" of the nation. Texas Christian University began to sponsor a Van Cliburn International Piano Competition every fourth year, and the famous pianist served as the host of the quadrennial event every year until his death. He did continue to tour, and played for every American president from Kennedy to Barack Obama, but his fame waned in the 1970s. He retired from public life in 1978 after the death of his father, although he did perform on special occasions.

Van Cliburn was a reluctant hero of the Cold War, a stature for which he never asked. A gentle man of great talent, who would still occasionally play the piano for his home church of Broadway Baptist in Fort Worth, he became the embodiment of the maturity of American culture during a tension-filled era.

Allan Shivers, the Tidelands, and the 1952 Governor's Race

TEXAS POLITICS CAN BE A RAUCOUS AFFAIR, and it certainly is not for the faint of heart. Texas politics, in the mid-twentieth century, had one of the deepest political fights in its history. From the 1940 through most of the 1970s these battles usually reflected the conservative/liberal divide present in the state's Democratic Party. At least through the 1950s the conservatives tended to be the remnants of what during the early twentieth century were called "business progressives" as well as those who had broken with Franklin Roosevelt and the national Democrats over portions of the New Deal. The liberal faction consisted of ardent New Dealers and many who called themselves "loyalists" because they remained true to the national party. The rancorous infighting between these two groups in the immediate postwar years produced some very vitriolic primaries, but in 1952 Allan Shivers would emerge from a governor's race as one of the most powerful men to ever occupy the office.

Robert Allan Shivers, born in Lufkin and raised in Woodville, would serve as the student association president at the University of Texas and after law school he became a quick rising star in Texas politics. At only thirty-nine he was elected Lieutenant Governor, and after the death of Governor Beauford Jester became the governor of Texas in 1949. First as lieutenant governor and then as governor Shivers pushed for business friendly policies, such as right-to-work laws, improvement of state highways, and higher taxes in order to build greater infrastructure and more money for higher and public education. In many ways, Shivers was a throwback to the "business progressivism" of the early twentieth century since he was not as frugal and unbending as more doctrinaire conservatives of his day, although there was no mistaking that Shivers was firmly in the conservative camp of the party.

Shivers finished Jester's term and then won another two years in 1950. When he filed to run for re-election in 1952 there was some controversy since no governor in the state's history had ever served more than two terms (four years). A Shivers victory would mean he would live in the Governor's Mansion for five years. His opponent, and the liberal faction stalwart, would be Austin district judge Ralph Yarborough. Although he had lost a race for attorney general in 1938, Yarborough's name was not well known to most Texans, which meant he had an uphill battle.

As the race for the 1952 governor's chair began, many Texans had another issue on their mind. For years Texas had engaged the federal government in a fight over its "tidelands," or the land that extends from the coast out to where national—or state, in this case—jurisdiction ends. Texas, on the basis that it had entered the Union by treaty because it was first an independent nation, had for years claimed jurisdiction over sea land out to three leagues, or just over ten miles. The U.S. had for years recognized this Texas right, but when oil was discovered on those lands in the 1930s the U.S. claimed jurisdiction. Texas and the U.S. fought for years in the courts over the controversy, but in 1948 President Harry Truman ordered his justice department to exercise control over the lands. Texas, once again, filed suit, but suffered a loss in the Supreme Court in 1949. Congress passed a law in 1952 once again giving such control to states, but President Truman vetoed the bill.

The Texas tidelands debate entered national politics during the 1952 presidential race, and it would eventually effect the Texas governor's contest. Dwight Eisenhower, the Republican nominee, came out in favor of allowing Texas to retain its sea lands, but the Democratic nominee, Adlai Stevenson, toed the Truman administration line and stated that he would not honor the Texas claim. Allan Shivers directly asked Stevenson if he would issue a quitclaim granting Texas the lands if he became president. When he refused, Shivers announced that he could not support the Democratic nominee and threw his support behind Eisenhower. He even went as far to organize a "Democrats for Eisenhower" organization and campaigned for the former general. Shivers' about face shocked many political pundits and professionals; support for a Republican would normally be anathema for most Texas Democrats, but the election would show that Shivers had guessed correctly.

Ralph Yarborough tried to make the governor's race a traditionally Texas liberal/conservative contest. He supported Truman, the New Deal and Fair Deal, and the goals and aspirations of the national party. Shivers, however, campaigned on the Tidelands and Texas "standing up" to the national government. When he, with legislative support, pledged that all the Tidelands royalties would go to Texas schoolchildren, Yarborough had few ways to counter the groundswell of popular support for the sitting governor. In the end, Shivers soundly beat Yarborough in the primary. Dwight Eisenhower would also win the presidential election, and one of his first acts was to make sure Texas retained ownership of its Tidelands.

Allan Shivers would go on to win an unprecedented third full term in 1954, once again over Yarborough. After he left the governor's mansion he would remain a key power broker in Texas conservative politics, as well as a prominent businessman and banker. He would be the longest serving Texas governor until current office holder Rick Perry surpassed his time in office in 2009.

Cooley and Debakey: Two Innovative Surgeons Made Houston a "Heart" Capital

I SUPPOSE THE HEART IS THE "ENGINE" of the human body—if it ceases to work life no longer exists. For years, any disease of the heart was essentially a death sentence, a fate in which medical science could neither reverse nor repair. What that meant was that millions of people died each year when their hearts became diseased or—as my grandmother used to say—"just gave out." While heart disease is still the leading cause of death in the U.S., it is not as large a leader in 2014 as it was fifty years ago, and a primary reason for that was the work of two Houston physicians, Michael E. Debakey and Denton A. Cooley.

Debakey was from Lake Charles, Louisiana, and he received his BA (1929) and M.D. (1932) degrees from Tulane University in New Orleans. He was immediately recognized as a rising star in the medical profession, particularly after completing surgical fellowships at the University of Strasbourg in France, and at the University of Heidelberg in Germany. He returned to his native Louisiana in 1939 to serve on the faculty of Tulane's medical school, and while there he was part of a team that made one of the first connections between cigarettes and lung cancer. During World War II he was one of the developers of the U.S. Army's innovative Mobile Army Surgical Hospital (MASH) units, and also established the Veteran's Administration Medical Center Research System.

After the war he joined the faculty of Baylor University College of Medicine (now known as Baylor College of Medicine), an institution that he would remain affiliated with until his death in 2008. Debakey quickly established himself as perhaps the leading vascular surgeon in the nation (the *Journal of the American Medical Association* wrote in 2005 that "many consider Michael E. Debakey to be the greatest surgeon ever"), and he was a pioneer in developing surgical procedures for bypassing blocked arteries in the neck, legs, and heart—techniques that are now studied and used extensively by virtually all vascular surgeons. He would also discover that Dacron grafts were excellent substitutes for damaged parts of arteries, a discovery that allowed surgeons to repair aorta and abdomen aneurysms that were previously inoperable.

He would gain his greatest fame as the "rebuilder of hearts." He pioneered the use of the coronary bypass to allow diseased hearts to continue to function, which he claimed to have performed in 1964, although he did not report it until a decade later. Debakey came under much criticism for his perceived flamboyance, and some medical professionals claimed he exaggerated his accomplishments, but what cannot be denied is his pioneer efforts at developing an artificial human heart.

After Dr. Christian Barnard performed the first human heart transplant in 1967 in South Africa, Debakey also began to perform the procedure. He and his medical team became the first ones to transplant four organs—a heart, two kidneys, and a lung—from one donor to different receipients. But he quickly surmised that the supply of suitable hearts for transplant would far outstrip the supply, thus if he could build an artificial heart then he could solve the problem. He first developed a partial artificial heart, a ventricular assist device (VAD), which he used to wean a woman from a heart-lung machine in 1966. He removed the device when the woman's heart function improved, and the woman lived for several more years. He had become the most recognizable heart surgeon in the country, and his VAD showed promise toward becoming a component in the quest to build a fully artificial heart, but he probably had no idea that the search for such an innovation would lead to a highly public "feud" with a former friend and team member—Denton Cooley.

Denton Cooley was a native Texan, born and raised in Houston. After graduating from the University of Texas, Cooley went to medical school at Johns Hopkins, where he graduated in 1944. He began to specialize in cardiovascular surgery, and then turned his focus almost solely to surgery on the heart. He gained a reputation as not only skilled but also operating with speed, a vital talent when surgically treating the heart. His status lead Michael Debakey to recruit him to Baylor and its associated Methodist Hospital in 1951. Eager to return to his home state, Colley accepted the invitation. In the end, their relationship had both triumph and then a prominent rift.

From Debakey, Cooley learned his mentor's innovative technique of removing aortic aneurysms. Debakey also shared with Cooley his ideas on building a heart-lung bypass machine. However, Cooley, while acknowledging Debakey's role, independently developed new surgical techniques, and also built his own heart-lung machine. When his version was chosen over Debakey's for use at Methodist Hospital their relationship became strained. Eventually, in 1960 Cooley moved from Methodist to another Houston medical leader, St. Luke's Episcopal Hospital, although he continued to teach at Baylor.

Cooley continued to work on developing artificial heart valves, with the ultimate goal of a fully functional artificial heart. He also began to study and learn Dr. Barnard's heart transplant techniques, and he performed his first transplant in May 1968. Cooley transplanted the heart of a fifteen year old suicide victim into a forty-seven year old man, who would live for 204 additional days. Within the next year he would perform twenty-two more transplants.

Cooley became the most innovative heart-transplant surgeon in the nation, but the quest for an artificial heart remained. In 1969, at great risk but desperate because no heart was available for a patient, Cooley implanted an artificial heart in to a dying patient. The artificial heart functioned for 65 hours until a human heart became available. It was rudimentary—Debakey called the procedure a "stunt"—but Cooley had proved that an artificial heart was possible. However, Debakey accused Cooley of stealing his research—a charge he denied—but the feud caused him to end his affiliation with Baylor.

Both men would continue to make innovations and save lives with their talent well after many professionals had retired. Debakey continued to work and research until he was near ninety, and Cooley continues to occasionally play his upright bass, and still advises surgeons in Houston. And the feud? It also ended. These two remarkably talented medical professionals reconciled in 2007, just before Debakey's death in 2008.

Lee Harvey Oswald's "Other" Victim

SOME DATES ARE SEARED INTO OUR CONSCIOUSNESS like a branding iron, so much that the very mention of them immediately brings to mind the seminal event associated with it. November 22, 1963 is just such a date. The murder of John F. Kennedy was a pivotal event in our history, one so significant that an entire generation knows *exactly* what they were doing when they heard the news. Some have said it was at that precise moment—12:30 P.M. CST—that America lost its innocence. Kennedy became a martyr—with good reason—but he was not the only person Lee Harvey Oswald gunned down that day. His second victim was Dallas Police Officer J.D. Tippit.

A son of East Texas born in Clarksville in 1924, Tippit joined the United States Army in 1944 as a member of the 513th Parachute Infantry Regiment of the 17th Airborne Division. He fought across France, and was part of the American forces that crossed the Rhine River in March 1945. He received a number of commendations, including the Bronze Star, and remained in the army until June 1946. When he returned home he married his high school sweetheart Marie Gasway in December 1946, and they would eventually have three children.

It is often difficult for veterans to adjust to civilian life, and it was even more demanding for Tippit, who was only nineteen when he entered the service. He first went to work for the Dearborn Stove Company as a technician, and in 1948 he became an appliance installer for Sears, Roebuck. He left that job in 1949 to return to his rural roots, becoming a cattle raiser on a small plot near Lone Star. That also did not turn out to be the career path for the young man from Red River County, and he was eager for something else. The United States government had established a number of programs to help veterans find employment and opportunities in peace-time society, so Tippit took advantage of one. He enrolled in a VA training school in Bogata in 1950, and after two years of study in law enforcement he found work as a patrolman for the Dallas Police Department. The twenty-eight year old former Airborne soldier had finally found a calling.

He worked through the ranks of the DPD and was on duty in his patrol area when the shots rang out in Dealey Plaza. Superiors ordered him to move to the central Oak Cliff area as police tried to concentrate a search for the assassin in the central part of the city. He was driving slowly on East 10th Street shortly after 1:00 P.M. when he spotted a man who fit the description of the alleged assassin—slender, white male, 5 feet 10 inches tall and in his early 30s. Tippit pulled up alongside the man he saw and asked him to step over to his patrol car. He talked with the suspect through an open window in the car, and at some point he asked the man to move back and allow him to exit. As he stepped out of his car and began to walk toward the front of the vehicle, Lee Harvey Oswald pulled a .38 caliber revolver from his pants and shot Tippit three times in the chest. The initial shots did not kill the thirty-nine year old officer, so Oswald coolly walked to where he had fallen and at point-blank range shot the officer in the head.

Witnesses reported that Oswald fled the scene and walked through an exit into the nearby Texas Theater. Police moved into the theater and surrounded the alleged assassin. Oswald pointed his gun at one officer's head as he moved to detain him, but the hammer on the revolver came down on the officer's hand instead of making contact with the chamber. Police quickly subdued the gunman and arrested him for the murder of Officer J.D. Tippit, not the President. At that time, the Dallas Police were not sure that this was the assassination's suspect.

Dallas rallied around Tippit's widow and the three children he left behind. A fund in the slain officer's honor raised more than $600,000 for the family in the years immediately following Tippit's murder. President Lyndon Johnson called to give his condolences, and

Jacqueline Kennedy sent a letter to Mrs. Tipitt expressing her extreme grief. The slain officer's funeral occurred on the same day as President Kennedy's—and Lee Harvery Oswald's.

For the record, and I do this because some folks will no doubt wonder, I believe that Lee Harvey Oswald was a lone assassin who killed President Kennedy. Conspiracy theories abound, but they tend to use selective evidence and leave out items that do not support their ideas. For me, the evidence against Oswald is just too strong, and one of the most compelling parts of that record is the shooting of J.D. Tippit. Why would Oswald shoot a policeman in such a cold-blooded fashion unless he knew that he was about to be charged with the "crime of the century?" For me, that tends to speak loudly.

No matter your beliefs on the assassination of John F. Kennedy, it was a national tragedy that became a transformative event in American history. For J.D. Tippit's family it is a day they will also never forget, but probably for a different reason than everyone else.

A Conversation With the Last Democratic Senator from Texas

ROBERT (BOB) KRUEGER DELIVERED a public address in Nacogdoches at Stephen F. Austin State University in October 2016 as part of the East Texas Historical Association's Georgiana and Max Lale Lecture series. I had the chance to extensively speak with the former senator and learned a number of fascinating aspects about this talented and remarkable man.

Given his distinguished and diverse career, anything that relates to Bob's life would be rich with detail and significant; his experiences dealing with the Rwandan genocide is exquisitely detailed in his book—co-written with his wife Kathleen—titled *From Bloodshed to Hope in Burandi:* Our Embassy Years during Genocide. While Krueger's encounter's in Africa were certainly significant and have proved to be the greatest example—though by no means the only—of his immense humanitarianism, I was fascinated by his accounts of Texas politics in the 1970s through the 1990s, primarily because they demonstrated how much the style and philosophy of policy and political interaction have changed in our state.

I jokingly referred to Bob as a living relic. I did so because he is the only person currently extant who can claim to have been a U.S. Senator from Texas as a Democrat. Governor Ann Richards appointed Krueger to fill Lloyd Bentsen's seat after he became the Secretary of the Treasury under President Bill Clinton. He sat in that chair until 1994, when Kay Bailey Hutchison, who had defeated him in a special election, took over. After leaving the senate, Krueger began his career with the State Department as an Ambassador, which led him to his life-altering mission in Africa.

Kruger may have served in the Senate in the 1990s, but he almost became a member of that body in the late 1970s when he became very close to defeating the incumbent Republican Senator John Tower in 1978. The New Braunfels native had entered Texas politics during the 1974 election when he came back to Texas from an academic career, and won a congressional seat as the representative from the sprawling Texas 21st district. He would serve two terms in one of the most conservative districts in the state, and was named by more than one publication as the "most effective Representative in the House." Kruger next decided to throw his hat into the arena for the Senate in 1978, but he lost the race to Tower by the razor-thin margin of just over 12,000 votes out of almost 2.3 million cast. In fact, he would have probably won the election had not the La Raza Unida candidate, Luis A Diaźde Leon, not polled a little over 20,000, votes that the vast majority would normally had gone to the Democrat.

Krueger spoke about what Washington—and particularly Congress—was like when he served. The most striking reality of that period was just how strong the Texas delegation was at the time. Texas congressman held five committee chairmanships, including those of powerful committees such as Appropriations and the Calendar. Men such as Omar Burleson, George Mahon, Wright Patman, and Bill Poage were some of the most powerful men in the House, and the seniority system gave them unprecedented control over legislation and policy. Krueger, remarking on serving as a junior Texas congressman during that time, said that he felt like a "prince among kings" because they were so respected.

Krueger also told how the "tone" of Congress was different then. During his first term, he helped to sponsor a bill that would remove many of the restrictions on the price of natural gas when it was shipped across state lines. Such policy hindered Texas operators—particularly the small independent producers—so Krueger was committed to ending the practice. However, many of the members of his own party, including the powerful Majority Leader and later Speaker of the House

"Tip" O'Neil, opposed his efforts. Such opposition did not deter the 21st representative, and he reached across the aisle and secured the support of many Republicans, as well as help form the Gerald Ford administration, to secure passage. The point, as Krueger drove home, was that bi-partisanship was much more the norm in those days, and was not seen as a "sign of weakness" or "betrayal" as it so often was today. Much like Congressman Charlie Wilson said often, Krueger also blamed the growth of extreme partisanship on the fallout from the 1994 election when after the Republicans gained control of Congress leaders such as Newt Gingrich began to force party loyalty with an iron hand.

Krueger also thought that the voters were different. They understood that the nation's welfare came first, and while they might be opposed in ways to certain policy, they also knew that compromise and reason were needed. During his first term, he agreed to speak in favor of Barbara Jordan's bill that would extend the Voting Rights Act to Texas. He knew that perhaps some in his district would oppose his actions—and Bob Poage told him he would not be reelected if he did so—but he had also vowed to make sure that no one in Texas should be denied the vote because they were not part of the majority. He supported the bill and still won re-election with over 70% of his district's vote. As he explained, "The people in my district were conservative, but they were not racist."

During his lecture Krueger urged his audience to not allow ideology to suppress anyone's humanity or compassion. He also wished to once again to see the majority of public servants practice principle over partisanship, and decency over the protection of privilege. I just wish we could once again have more people like Robert Krueger in public service.

II: Places

The Road From the North: Trammel's Trace

NACOGDOCHES' CLAIM TO BEING THE oldest town in Texas rests, predominantly, on the fact that the location of the present-day city has been continuously populated since Spanish Captain Domingo Ramón led an expedition to the former site of a Hasinai Caddo village that established Mission Nuestra Señora De Guadalupe de Nacogdoche in 1716. The trail from Presidio San Juan Bautista on the Rio Grande that Ramón followed would eventually be known as El Camino Real, and it would be the primary Spanish transportation conduit through the Frontéra Norteña, a road that connected Mexico City to Coahuila, San Antonio, Nacogdoches, and on to Los Ades near the French town of Natchitoches in Louisiana. Presently, the remnants of the El Camino Real in Nacogdoches run closely to what we call Main Street and State Highway 21.

During the time Nacogdoches was under the dominion of first the Spanish and then the Republic of Mexico, it was one of tonly two "cities" in Texas, with the other being San Antonio. In a pattern that continues into the twenty-first century, the fortunes of a city depended greatly on the access it had to the outside world. Nacogdoches prospered because of it prominence on the major road; El Camino Real made Nacogdoches the "entry point," if you will, to Texas, and thus if you had traveled to Texas east through Louisiana—a popular route—you followed the El Camino Real from Natchitoches to the Sabine, crossed at what eventually became known as Gaines Ferry, then continued to Nacogdoches. If you were going farther, you left Nacogdoches and went south on El Camino Real to San Antonio and perhaps points farther south.

One well-traveled and important road can make a city viable, but two that crossed in a city made it significant and, in the years of a frontier, helped make it permanent and prosperous since the location where roads crossed became a gathering spot for people. To use a contemporary phrase, El Camino Real helped put Nacogdoches on the map, but another road—Trammel's Trace—made Nacogdoches a strategic and important city within Spain and later Mexico. If you were traveling to Texas from the northeast, such as coming from anywhere north of the Deep South states, you traversed Missouri or Arkansas, and then crossed into Texas much north of El Camino Real. The road you began to make your journey on in Arkansas was Trammel's Trace.

Trammel's Trace, like the El Camino Real, most likely existed as a Caddo trade route long before whites used it to travel into Texas. Early Anglo filibusterers, such as Philip Nolan, used the trace as their entry point into Spanish Texas for their illegal activities. The Trace had no name until the 1820s. Nicholas Trammel, a Tennessean who fled that state to Arkansas to escape gambling debts, and perhaps a theft charge, opened a tavern in Arkansas, but his old habits returned and he spent most of his time racing horses and running gambling games. Trammel traveled the northern route to Texas for match races against Texas ponies. He and Daniel Davis, in 1824, widened and improved the trail so that it could handle wagons and supply carts for migrants now making a steady stream toward Mexican Texas. Eventually, the route gained his name: Trammel's Trace.

Travelers could enter the Trace at Fulton, Arkansas to travel the longest route, but the majority of travelers used other routes and joined the Trace at Pecan Point, Arkansas. It then ran south and crossed seven present East Texas counties. It went from Pecan Point to Stephenson's Crossing on the Sulphur River and then entered Texas just below the Red River. It then ran to a crossing on the Sabine near the intersection of current Rusk, Panola, and Harrison Counties. After crossing the Sabine, it continued south-southwest to Nacogdoches to its intersection with El Camino Real, approximately at the current crossroad of North and Main Streets. Luminaries such as David Crockett and Sam Houston most likely came to Nacogdoches via Trammel's Trace.

Trammel's Trace, combined with El Camino Real made Nacogdoches the second most important, and second largest town in Texas at the time the Texas Revolution. It is a noteworthy part of Texas history that, in my opinion, has not gotten its proper due. That has begun to change in recent years. Texas A&M Press, in 2016, published Gary Pinkerton's *Trammel's Trace: The First Road to Texas From the North*. The book quickly made a stir and revived interest in the old route. That led Nacogdoches's Stone Fort Chapter of the Daughter's of the Republic of Texas to initiate a campaign to place a monument to honor the route. The results of that campaign will now become reality as the DRT will have a ceremony dedicated a Trammel's Trace Monument on Tuesday October 2, 2018, at 10:00 A.M. at the "Hitch Lot" (Farmer's Market) on Pearl Street, near the historic crossroad of Trammel's Trace and the El Camino Real. The public is invited to help honor this commemoration of making Nacogdoches the "Crossroads of Texas."

A Gateway to Texas

TODAY'S HIGHWAYS, BYWAYS, BRIDGES, and interstates mean that most of us never think about the difficulty of travel in the days before such modern conveniences. During the days of our great-great grandparents a journey of just twenty miles, depending on conditions, could take days and involve much toil and anxious moments. Rivers especially posed a serious impediment to travel; they tended to flood, could contain treacherous, shifting currents, and often had inaccessible banks. Bridges were expensive and difficult to build, and their maintenance demanded constant attention. Thus, ferry operations became a vital and important part of the nation's transportation system of the nineteenth century.

Most travelers to Texas in the early to mid-1800s came from the United States; some made their way by ship and thus disembarked along the coast, but those who came overland usually found a route to the terminus of the El Camino Real in Natchitoches, Louisiana and then traveled that road into Texas. Such a route required one to cross the Sabine River, a waterway that in the 1820s and 1830s was wide, often swift, and had very few natural places to cross. The El Camino Real crossed the Sabine at what was originally known as Chabanan Ferry, but by the 1820s migrants to Texas knew it as Gaines Ferry, so named after its owner and operator James Gaines.

James Gaines came from a very prominent and distinguished family in Virginia. He joined his cousin, American Army officer Edmund Pendleton Gaines, in an expedition west to survey the lands along the Natchez Trace in 1803. Both men would eventually make their lives and careers in the West, Edmund as a prominent military commander in Louisiana, and James as an entrepreneur and businessman in western Louisiana. The two cousins also became involved in intrigue along the border. Edmund had a role in numerous "filibustering" expeditions into Texas in the early 1800s (including the famous Phillip Nolan excursion), and James help to raise men and served as an officer in the Republican Army of the North (RAN) in 1810-1811. The RAN would march across the border and first occupy Nacogdoches before turning south to San Antonio and a date with infamy. A Spanish royal army under General Joquin Arrendondo first defeated the RAN at the Battle of the Medina River, and then ordered the execution of any associated with the insurrection. James Gaines luckily escaped the fate of death that befell so many members of the RAN and went back to Virginia for a while where he fought against the British in the War of 1812.

James Gaines' passion remained in the West—it was where he believed his fortune lay—so he returned to the border area where his cousin was now the commander of U.S. Fort Jessup. James was not the only American who had decided that the west was a land of economic opportunity in the years after the War of 1812 and into the 1820s. Hundreds of thousands of his fellow countrymen traveled the roads into the Louisiana Purchase lands. Many of them—some of them quite illegally—began to cross the border into what was now Mexican Texas in the mid 1820s. Chaos in Mexico had prevented that new nation was establishing any control over its northern border, so countless Americans took advantage of the condition and came to Texas to squat and hope for a title at a later date. James Gaines saw an opportunity and seized it.

The new Texas migrants needed a way across the river, so James Gaines bought the ferry that crossed the Sabine along the El Camino Real. Along with his sons he operated the business, and also built and opened a general store, a tavern and inn for the many travelers that passed through, and speculated in land. He became a prominent citizen of the region and would serve as alcalde for the Sabine District of the Municipality of Nacogdoches, the Nacogdoches sheriff, and the postmaster for the area. He also became very involved in leading the opposition to Haden Edwards during the Fredonian Rebellion in 1827. Later, he would become embroiled in the political debates in the region that eventually lead to the Texas Revolution.

Gaines Ferry became the most used and recognizable port of entry for Texas in the 1830s. After independence, the ferry location on the Texas side of the Sabine became the town of Pendleton (probably named after James Gaines' military leader cousin), and the new Republic of Texas made it a customs collection port in 1837. Gaines sold the ferry to a group of businessmen in 1843 and moved to Nacogdoches, although the crossing would retain his name. The ferry remained a profitable and important part of the transportation infrastructure of East Texas throughout the nineteenth century, although its fortunes declined with the arrival of the railroad and modern bridges. Eventually, the Pendleton-Gaines Bridge replaced the ferry in 1937.

The next time you make your way east on Hwy. 21 and reach the border, take a minute to look around and imagine that you found not a nice, modern bridge but instead a wooden ferry with a rope and pulley system. And then know that you would have been very glad to find Gaines Ferry in operation.

Mexican Sentinel in East Texas: Fort Teran

NEWS SHOWS, TALK PROGRAMS, AND NEWSPAPERS are filled today with stories and arguments about illegal, or undocumented, immigration. Immigration controversy is not a twentieth or twenty-first century phenomenon to our state; it has raged before and it will continue to rage in the future. Such is the nature of a borderland. It was just as large an issue, and a potentially more dangerous one, in the 1820s, only then it was Mexico worrying about the political and cultural impacts of Americans illegally crossing the border.

Texas passed to Mexico after the end of the Mexican War for Independence in 1821. Other than missions and scattered outposts (such as Nacogdoches), Spain had never been able to truly populate Texas; there were too few reasons for Mexicans to leave the interior of Mexico and travel to the nation's far off, mostly unknown, and perilous northern frontier. Mexico, like colonial Spain before it, faced a quandary—how to populate their northern frontier but also retain sovereignty.

The primary problem was that while the residents of the interior of Mexico had no real desire to move to the *fronteria norteno*, there were some folks who did—Anglo Americans. They had begun to cast their eyes on Mexico's northern reaches in fits of Manifest Destiny and Jacksonian expansion, and something as intangible as a national border was not near enough to stop their advance. Perhaps Mexico realized resistance was futile. Perhaps they decided to take the easiest and most inexpensive course of action. Perhaps they were just short sighted. For whatever reason, Mexico decided to allow a program of Anglo immigration into Texas. It began with Stephen F. Austin as the first *empresario*, but he was not the only one who entered into contracts with Mexican authorities to place American settlers in Texas. The contracts expressly required the new settlers to become Mexican citizens and follow Mexican laws. For the most part, the new settlers did so—at least publicly.

The problem for Mexico was that for almost every legal migrant to Texas one illegal "squatter" also came to the province. Most of these congregated near the American border around Nacogdoches, and they also saw no reason to give up their American culture and assimilate. They just transported the American customs, language, law, and social ideas to their new home, never caring that they had entered a new nation with its own unique customs, laws, language, and ideas.

Mexico had its own internal problems during the era, most particularly in deciding what sort of government they wished to establish and dealing with all the accoutrements that come with the implementation of a new nation. That meant they had no real idea what was happening on the northern reaches of their nation until Manual Mier y Teran made an inspection tour of Texas and issued a report. What Teran found appalled him—an entire region almost void of any semblance of Mexican authority or custom. By 1830 he had convinced the Mexican government to act, and one of their new strictures was to end all immigration from Mexico. That meant some sort of force and structure had to enforce Mexican law.

Most illegal American immigrants entered Mexican Texas from the east, so any military installation to stop such a flow had to be in East Texas. Teran was placed in charge of enforcing the law, and he instructed Peter Ellis Bean to locate and build a fort upon a suitable site. Bean chose to build what would become Fort Teran near a ridge on the Neches River where three different trails from the east met to cross the river. That site is now in Tyler County, about a half-mile downstream from the mouth of Shawnee Creek, three miles west of Rockland.

Construction of the fort was difficult and suffered from a lack of labor, materials, and funding. Colonel Jose de las Piedras, the commander of the garrison at Nacogdoches, continually appealed to Mexico City for carpenters and supplies that in most cases never arrived. Eventually, Fort Teran consisted of no more than ten small cabins, perhaps a rudimentary picket, and never housed more than one hundreds troops in its garrison. Its effectiveness in stopping the tide of illegal immigration was also dubious; almost as many Americans came to Texas after 1831 as did in the whole decade before. The fact was that Mexican authority was tenuous in Texas, and authorities in the province had little hope of actually enforcing the law. In many cases they had no desire to; East Texas was much closer to the United States than it was to Mexico City and depended on trade with Louisiana, Missouri, and the rest of the American South for its livelihood.

Hostilities between Mexican authority and Anglo settlers eventually reached a boiling point. After actions at Anahuac and Velasco on the coast, and in Nacogdoches in the early 1830s, Mexican troops abandoned Fort Teran in 1834. The old site supported a trading post and a ferry for a while, and later a post office. By the 1870s, most of the site was in ruins and the old fort unused. Today there are no remnants that remain of what was once the isolated Mexican sentinel among the churning pot of cultural clash in East Texas. But it does make you realize that immigration and all it entails is more than a political issue. Forcing culture on a people usually does not work. If history teaches us anything it is that assimilation must be gradual and voluntary, and simply drawing a line at an arbitrary border does not solve all problems in a borderland.

A Forgotten Town: Independence, TX

A TRIP MADE ME REMEMBER THAT WACO was not the first home to Baylor, one of the premier private institutions in the state, and perhaps the most notable Baptist affiliated university in the nation. Instead the honor of the founding place for Baylor goes to a small town that today has barely more than one hundred residents—Independence, a Washington County hamlet just a short distance from Bryan-College Station.

The land that would eventually constitute Independence was part of Stephen F. Austin's original grant that brought the "Old Three-Hundred" to Texas. J.G.W. Pierson, Robert Stevenson, Colbert Baker, and Amasa F. Burchard founded the town on thirty-five acres of the grant in 1835. The town rapidly grew and within ten years was a significant settlement that claimed to be the wealthiest community in Texas.

Commerce was important, but it was religion, specifically the Baptists, that shaped and formed Independence in the mid-nineteenth century. Thomas W. Cox and Thomas Spraggins organized the Independence Baptist Church in 1839, a congregation that is still active and is the second-oldest church affiliated with the Baptist General Convention. Sam Houston became a member of Independence Baptist when he decided to make his wife Margaret happy and agree to be baptized at Rocky Creek in 1854. When Pastor Rufus Burleson told the old general that "all your sins are now washed away," Houston reportedly replied, "Lord help the fish down below."

And it was again the Baptists that really made Independence a Texas city of note when, in 1845, the Baptist Educational Society chose Independence as the site of their new institution of higher learning, a college that would eventually become Baylor University. Named after one of its founders R.E.B. Baylor, the school began as a coeducational institution, but in 1851 officially divided into male and female departments. It would be only the male school that would go on to be designated Baylor University. The female school would eventually move to Belton and take its present name, the University of Mary Hardin-Baylor.

Baylor was only the beginning of Independence's growth and prosperity. Through the 1850s the town added a hotel, a stagecoach depot, a new, shiny, modern jail, and a Masonic lodge. It became the center of Washington County business activity, eclipsing the prominence of its neighbors Washington-on-the-Brazos and Brenham. Some even began to refer to Independence as the "Athens of Texas," and it seemed poised to become one of the most important cities in the state.

Very often things do not work out as planned, and such was the case for Independence when they made the same fateful decision that doomed many cities and towns in the mid-nineteenth century. Officials with the Santa Fe Railroad came to Independence in the early 1870s and made an offer they thought would not be refused. If the town and the university would donate land and grant other concessions for a right-of-way, then the track would come right through the center of the city. A railroad, they argued, would cement Independence as a "great" town and assure its future growth and distinction. The Santa Fe people believed it was a sure offer, but the town's officials, supported by the university's administrators, spurned the railroad. The Santa Fe built around Independence, eventually laying its track through Brenham, which made Independence's Washington County competitor the most important town in the county.

Independence slowly declined, but the real blow came in 1885. In that year, Baylor officials decided to move their institutions: Baylor University went to Waco, and Baylor Female College relocated to Belton. Today, Independence counts just over a hundred residents. The major highways have bypassed the little town, and it no longer has a post office. It does still contain some wonderful historic structures, such as the Margaret Houston House, and the Houston-Lea Cemetery, the final resting place of Margaret M.L. Houston. If you make the drive to the little place in the spring you will also be rewarded with some of the most colorful wildflowers in the state. A formerly important city that now rests sleepily in the countryside, almost forgotten.

A City Where the Decencies of Life Were Forgotten

SOME OF THE MOST NOTORIOUS AND DECADENT places within any area of the world lie at the fuzzy borders of a frontier, those places quite often defined most readily by the lack of social grace or any semblance of "law and order." Texas, and its borders, have had its share of such places, such as the "Neutral Ground" between Spanish Texas and American Louisiana in the early nineteenth century, the renowned city of Tascosa in the Panhandle where a number of outlaws and nefarious characters "holed up," and the many legendary (and it was more legend than fact) towns established around the frontier forts of the late 1800s. Another one of those infamous places was not actually in Texas, but Bagdad, Tamaulipas, Mexico—from which the title quote of this article references— a Mexican city at the mouth of the Rio Grande, played a significant role in Texas' Civil War era experience.

Bagdad's roots trace back to 1848 when it became a port to ferry Mexican troop supplies north during the opening stages of the U.S./Mexican War. As a port, it was not much at the time because the water around the coast was very shallow and ships could generally get no closer than about a hundred yards, which meant any goods or passengers had to be tendered to shore by smaller vessels. It struggled through most of its early days and by 1860 was not much more than a poor shanty town with just about a hundred residents.

The American Civil War changed Bagdad's fortunes. One of the primary Union strategies for winning the war was to make sure that the Confederacy was not able to take advantage of its cotton economy. Thus, the U.S. Navy blockaded the Confederate coastline, stopping any ocean-going conveyance that might transport goods bound from or to a CSA port. However, Mexico was a neutral nation in the struggle between North and South, which meant that the federal blockade did not extend to south of Texas. Furthermore according to international legal precedent, the Rio Grande, since it served as an international border, was off limits to the U.S. blockade. That made Bagdad a valuable piece of real estate.

During the earliest stages of the Civil War, it was primarily Texas cotton that found its way to Bagdad. Richard King, the founder of the King Ranch, who had originally made his fortune in trade along the Rio Grande in the 1840s, returned to his commercial roots during the Civil War when he shipped tons of cotton around the world out of Bagdad. Soon, cotton carts and wagons carrying not only Texas cotton by those of other southern states began to fill the brush country of South Texas—all headed to the little port on the south bank of the Rio Grande. Ships anchored in the water just off Bagdad's shore, all trying to get in line to load cotton for transport throughout the world. It did not take long for the process to bog down since there were not near enough carts, small ships, and labor to service the hundreds of thousands of cotton bales that arrived weekly in the small city. It could take as long as two months to load a single schooner with cotton by late 1862, and with the fall of Vicksburg in the summer of 1863, when Bagdad became the chief cotton export town for the Confederacy, the wait for a load grew to as long as four months. The Confederacy even began to use some of the camels brought to Texas in the 1850s for use at the Texas frontier forts to load cotton. Ironically, it was Jefferson Davis, when he was U.S. Secretary of War, who had pioneered the utilization of camels in Texas. Davis, of course, was in the 1860s the president of the Confederate States of America.

Boom towns, be they spurred by gold, oil, or in this case shipping, tend to take on predictable patterns. Great economic upheavals bring a certain "character" to a region, one who is usually adventurous, sometimes aggressive, and certainly willing to take a risk. While such characteristics often serve an entrepreneur well in a boom town, when they extend to personal habits it can breed behavior that is more, well, disreputable. Bagdad, and the people who migrated to the now burgeoning town, fit the traditional mold. Almost overnight the town grew from just a few hundred people to over 15,000, and the vast majority of that growth was young men. These men looked to activities traditionally associated with young men, so Bagdad became a town full of saloons, brothels, casinos, and opium dens. Gunplay on the streets was a nightly occurrence, and any attempt to enforce law and order was almost immediately overwhelmed by the sheer number of law breakers. The *New York Herald* famously described Bagdad as "an excrescence of the war, [a congregation] of blockade runners, desperadoes, the vile of both sexes, adventurers, [and] numberless groggeries and houses of worse fame." If you were looking to find someone who would entertain the notion of any scheme one might have—legal or not—Bagdad was a likely place to find one.

Then it was all over. When the Civil War ended, any importance of Bagdad as a port culminated with it. Ships would still occasionally visit, but the shortcomings that had limited it before the Civil War made it a less desirable port once again. It enjoyed some activity as a recreational outlet for both American and Mexican tourists wishing to enjoy the beach in the 1870s, but for the most part it was a dying town. By 1880 it was all but abandoned, and a hurricane in 1889 essentially wiped it out. Today, if you know where to look when you visit Boca Chica State Park at the mouth of the Rio Grande, just over the river you can still spot some of the old pilings on a very desolate beach, all that is left of the once bustling port of Bagdad.

The Loneliest Outpost on the Frontier

I WAS BORN IN ABILENE, which is in the middle of the rolling plains of Texas. We lived in the "Key City" until I was in the third grade, and my Dad loved to take the family on weekend drives into the countryside. One place we often drove past was a historic fort with a ghostly name: Fort Phantom Hill. All that was left of the old frontier post were lonely brick chimneys, and decaying foundations of what once were the buildings that housed the garrison of what many soldiers called the "loneliest outpost on the frontier." I am sure that much of it was the name, but when we passed by and saw those sentinel like specters, especially the one time we got out and walked among the old foundations and the chimneys, I was sure that I felt some sort of scary, ghostly presence. Of course, it may have also been the prominent sign that read, "Warning: Rattlesnakes present. Proceed with caution." Perhaps those old soldiers were also afraid of the presence of those slithering serpents.

When the United States annexed Texas in 1845, and then after the subsequent Mexican War, one of the obligations the nation undertook in Texas was to provide for frontier defense. One region that encompassed was along the Mexican border, where the Treaty of Guadalupe Hidalgo tasked U.S. troops with stopping Native American raids into Mexico. The other military responsibility in Texas was two-fold: one was to protect the towns and settlements east of the "frontier line" from the same sort of attacks, and the other was to provide escort and protection for travelers, stage lines, and other treks that made their way through Texas to the west, which became more urgent after gold was discovered and the rush of wealth seekers headed to California traveled the rudimentary byways to that ultimate destination.

President Polk sent Captain Randolph B. Marcy on an expedition to explore and mark a suitable—and safe—route through Comanchería in Texas and New Mexico. Marcy first recommended, and helped establish a cordon of forts along the Rio Grande in 1849-1850, and then a second line, known as the "frontier defense line" that ran roughly north to south from Fort Worth to intersect with Fort Duncan near the Rio Grande. That frontier line worked so well that by 1851, Marcy staked out a second frontier line that would moved further west. The new frontier line would stretch also along that north/south direction, but this time beginning with Fort Belknap (near present day Newcastle), and then to near the Rio Grande and newly established Fort Clark, near present day Brackettville. Included in that line was Fort Phantom Hill.

Forts needed a reliable water source, and one of the key requirements was to find a suitable such stream. The original orders had called for the fort that would become Phantom Hill to be built near Pecan Bayou in what is now Coleman County. But, Lt. Colonel John J. Abercrombie, who was sent to establish the post, made the poor decision of discarding that recommendation and established the garrison instead at a spot near where Elm Creek intersected with the Clear Fork of the Brazos in present day Jones County. Abercrombie arrived at the spot with five companies of the Fifth Infantry on November 14, 1851. The Fifth was part of the newly organized Texas Eighth Military Department under the command of General William G. Belknap. Belknap was not well, so his immediate subordinate, General Persifor Smith signed off on Abercrombie's change of location.

He should not have. The alteration affected the post's effectiveness. The Clear Fork is an intermittent stream in the best of times, and when it does hold water it is often brackish, Elm Creek was usually dry, except for those rare occasions when much rain falls and it flooded everything in its expanded path. Also, this part of the Rolling Plains is almost devoid of adequate timber for building. The soldiers did establish a stone quarry two miles south of the fort, but any lumber for beams and posts had to brought in by ox wagon from more than forty miles away. One soldier, while the fort was being built, called the area a "barren waste."

Soldier life at the garrison was difficult. The water supply was always a problem, and a well the soldiers dug proved unreliable. The fort was also extremely isolated, which made it vulnerable to attack. And, because the army had chosen to post infantry at the fort instead of Cavalry, the soldiers were no match for the skilled horseman that manned the Comanche war parties. The fort also suffered from a lack of consistency in commanders, as in its short stint as a post (1851-1854) four men would serve in that capacity.

Shortly after the fort was established, its importance waned. The frontier was fairly well pacified by the establishment of Indian reservations and forts on the Upper Brazos. The frontier line had actually shifted, and the post was essentially not needed. The Army ordered the post abandoned on April 6, 1854, and the soldiers were mostly sent to Forts Belknap and McKavett. Mysteriously, shortly after the soldiers left, the fort buildings burned to the ground, leaving only those lonely foundations and chimneys. Also oddly enough, the fort was never officially named, just referred to by the soldiers as "Phantom Hill," probably due to the fact that from a distance it looks like the small "hill" the fort was built upon rises a considerable distance off the plains, but once you get to it, it is but a small knoll, barely rising above the surrounding ground. But part of me wants to believe that the name came from the lonely men who had to man this forsaken, isolated sentinel in West Texas.

Swept Away: The Story of Indianola

IF YOU JOURNEY TO CALHOUN COUNTY and travel down from Port Lavaca on the south side of Matagorda Bay, at low tide you can see something curious—some foundational ruins and what looks to be an old, ancient town out in the surf. A historical marker will let you know that you are standing at the former site of Indianola, once one of the most important ports and cities in Texas, but one that Gulf Coast hurricanes seemed to particularly target for destruction. Two different tropical cyclones destroyed the port town, and after the last one residents just gave up and never rebuilt.

The coastal area around what would become Indianola was an important landing spot on the Texas coast even before a town existed. Some of the "Old 300" settlers bound for Stephen F. Austin's colony landed on the beach at Matagorda Bay, and it was there Karl, Prince of Solms Braunfels chose as a landing spot for his German migrants who would move inland and found New Braunfels, beginning large-scale German immigration to Texas. The area became known as Indian Point, and it also became a key supply port for the United States Army during the Mexican War and after. It would be there that the army landed camels for the experiment of using the Asian animals as supply beasts in West Texas.

A town, also originally known as Indian Point, grew around the depot and the landing area. The U.S. government located a post office there in 1847 and the town began to expand as entrepreneurs bought lots, built businesses, and began to service and to supply the maritime industry along the coast. The town changed its name to

Indianola in 1849 and it became the seat of Calhoun County in 1852, an honor it would hold until its final destruction in 1886. Since it was a supply point for any excursions to West Texas, as well as a key immigrant landing site, by the 1860s only Galveston surpassed it as a Texas port.

The Gulf of Mexico is a violent body of water, a sea subject to quick developing storms that can grow to a monstrous size. Any city, settlement, or structure that sits on the Gulf Coast simply waits for the next storm and hopes it does not make a direct hit. Indianola's luck held out until 1875. The city was probably at the peak of its prosperity in that year; more than five thousand people called the port home, steamships routinely anchored and traded at its wharves, and since 1871 the railroad allowed goods and people to travel from Indianola into the interior. The science of weather prediction was not even remotely exact in the 1870s, and Gulf cities and its residents had little or no warning before cyclones raged inland. On September 15, 1875 a Gulf storm slammed into the crowded city. Water from the bay inundated Indianola's streets; the storm surge shifted buildings off the foundation and carried them away. What the water did not destroy the wind did. It was a particularly large and violent storm that became worse when it stalled out over the Texas coast, which caused it to rage for two days. Indianola was virtually destroyed. Only eight buildings were left standing and three hundred people had lost their lives.

The 1875 hurricane so devastated the town that it ensured Indianola would never be the city it once was. But it is difficult to "kill" a town that people call home and operate businesses, so many Indianolians decided to rebuild. Once again Indianola began to slowly become a key port, and after 1880s even began to lure back some of its former shippers and traders. But the Gulf can be fickle, and its towns remain targets for those deadly storms. Another one arrived on August 19, 1886, and it was larger and meaner than the 1875 cyclone. First-hand accounts tell of a storm surge that had to be at least in the ten-foot range, probably larger. To make matters worse, while the water and wind ravaged the town a fire broke out and burned what the storm did not annihilate. When the catastrophe ended, there was nothing left.

This time, Indianola could not recover. The residents who survived the storm either moved away from the coast or relocated to Port Lavaca, the main beneficiary of the Indianola's misfortune in 1875. Many towns often linger for a few years before they become "ghost towns,' but Indianola's demise was swift; by 1887 it no longer existed. Today, all that remains are those eerie foundations, a La Salle statue commemorating the presumed spot the French explorer waded to shore, an old dilapidated bridge, a historical marker, and a desolate stretch of Gulf sand. Perhaps such minimalism is fitting for the former important port that the violent Gulf of Mexico took back.

Mary Allen College: An Educational Beacon for African Americans

THE MOMENTOUS 1865 END OF SLAVERY in Texas brought freedom for roughly 200,000 people of African descent who had spent their lives in chattel bondage, but freedom did not ensure a future of equal opportunity, economic progress, or a guarantee of full civil rights. For that, African Americans would have to struggle mightily for more than a hundred more years—and in many ways such toil continues. The state's southern concept of white superiority and insistence on maintaining its racial "order" extended into almost every facet of African American life, with the effect of numerous roadblocks and obstacles to any semblance of a full flowering of American citizenship rights.

One considerable impediment to progress for blacks was the opportunity for a full education. Texas' segregated and dilapidated school system was poorly funded and haphazard at best, which prevented most African Texans from acquiring the very skills most needed to fight the conditions of a Jim Crow system—which was very often the aim of local white school districts. Black Texas leaders certainly understood the inadequacies of the system in which they were forced to live. Thus, during the late nineteenth century, black communities approached remedies with resolve, usually under the direction of African American church congregations. East Texas became a region blessed with a number of outstanding black higher education institutions, names familiar to modern ears such as Paul Quinn, Bishop, and Wiley Colleges. Mary Allen Junior College in

Crockett is a name perhaps less familiar to today's East Texan, but one that was every bit as vital as its more famous contemporaries.

What became Mary Allen Junior College in the twentieth century began as the Crockett Presbyterian Church Colored School in 1871. In 1875, it became known as Moffatt Parochial School. Like many black schools, the local congregation bore the full costs of construction and curriculum materials, a substantial sacrifice for church members who primarily depended on the vagaries of sharecrop farms for their livelihood. Eventually, with the aid of the Presbyterian Church, U.S.A. (Northern), and local Crockett businessmen, the Reverend Samuel Fisher Tenney was able to build a boarding school for African American young women. The name of the new school became the Mary Allen Seminary, named after the wife of the secretary of the Presbyterian U.S.A's Board of Missions for Freedmen.

With a newly constructed building on a ten-acre plot north of the city, the school began as a day and boarding school with classes at the primary, elementary, and high-school levels, as well as a teacher-training institution for women only. The school became successful and, under the direction of Reverend J.B. Smith, began to expand; by 1890 it consisted of two multi-storied buildings and enrolled more than two hundred students.

Smith resigned in 1910 and for the next decade Mary Allen Seminary began a decline in enrollment and funding. Clearly, the school needed a new direction. In 1924 Reverend Burt Randall Smith, the first black administrator, revitalized the institution. Reverend Smith brought in an all-black faculty, improved the school buildings and infrastructure, and began a more rigorous curriculum. The Texas State Department of Education granted the school accreditation as a high school in 1925, and in 1927 the first junior college class graduated. Eventually, the board eliminated the lower grades from the school and in 1933 it became Mary Allen Junior College and coeducational.

The new focus led the Presbyterian National Board of Missions to approve a proposal in 1942 to make Mary Allen a four-year state college for black students, but World II and the Texas legislature's indifference ended such dreams. In that year, the school closed but it did reopen in 1944 under the control of the Missionary Baptist Convention of Texas. Eventually, struggling to attract students and funding, the school closed in 1972.

African American students today have a plethora of educational options available, opportunities that their grandparents did not have just a few decades ago. But the dream of education as progress was always a part of the African American community and today's students owe a tribute to the perseverance of institutions such as Mary Allen Junior College. Perhaps a drive to Crockett and a look (and maybe a little reverence) at the ruins of this once proud educational beacon will remind them of the sacrifice past generations made for such advancement.

Protecting The Gulf: Fort Crockett

GALVESTON HAS TO BE ONE OF MY FAVORITE Texas cities. There is just something that begins change within me when I drive over that causeway or at the moment the Bolivar Ferry leaves its launch and ventures across the pass. I suppose it has something to do with the sea, or perhaps the romanticism of pirates, sea-going vessels, and arriving immigrants. Maybe a more likely reason is my passionate appreciation for all things Jimmy Buffet (yes, I am a Parrothead), but whatever it is, thinking of Galveston always makes me smile.

I came to my ardor for the island innocently as it was a destination for a family trip a few times in my younger days. During one of those trips I faintly remember a "snake show" housed in an imposing concrete structure that looked out across the Gulf of Mexico. Given my extreme fear of snakes I wanted nothing to do with any sort of reptile exhibition, but the concrete bunker intrigued me. I asked my Dad what it was and he told me that it was a part of old Fort Crockett, which protected the island from the Nazis during World War II.

I never forgot about Fort Crockett, and continued to look for that bunker every time I returned. And it's still there, although it no longer contains a "snake show," and the graffiti that once covered it has been scrubbed clean. Today it is a part of the San Luis Resort, and it has a swimming pool built directly on top of it. My wife and I recently visited the San Luis and the portion where we stayed was near one of the old bunkers, so close that I had the opportunity to walk up to it and touch the feet thick, reinforced concrete walls. I thought to myself, "yes, it would take a mighty piece of ordinance to crack these bulwarks"

What I did not know is that the bunker was not actually located at the primary facility of Fort Crockett. I also had no idea that the fort had a history that stretched back before World War II. The United States Army established Fort Crockett in the late 1890s, and it was still under construction when the Storm of 1900 devastated the island in September of that year. Finally finished in 1903, a Coast Guard artillery unit occupied the fort as the first "tenants" to provide a defense of the vital shipping lanes that moved petroleum and other products out of Galveston Bay.

World War I changed Fort Crockett's mission. In that war, there was not much danger of a seaborne attack or invasion, so the fort became an important artillery training center. It boasted some of the most modern weapons of the day, including ten-inch and rapid-fire guns. Eventually, the fort became the headquarters for the Sixty-ninth Coast Artillery; a unit of the Twentieth Coast Artillery also manned the facility and both were charged with harbor defense.

After the Great War, Fort Crockett became the home base of the United States Army Air Corps' 3rd Attack Group. The airplane had become a more important part of warfare first during and, most rapidly, directly following World War I. The 3rd Attack Group was the only American air squad devoted solely to attack aircraft. Galveston proved to be a good locale to train to fight in the sky; to be brutally honest, when a plane crashed over the ocean there was no danger of civilian casualties. However, salt air is not good for metal aircraft, so by the mid-1930s, the 3rd Group moved on to Barksdale, Louisiana.

World War II reinvigorated Fort Crockett's importance. The Army expanded its batteries and the focus became not training but protecting the Texas coast (and its vital oil facilities) from German U-boat attack. The huge bunkers, which housed the coastal guns, were constructed of thick concrete impervious to the bombing capabilities of invasive battalions. Those were the structures that so intrigued me in my youth.

After the war, when the Cold War meant that the U.S. would have to retain a large military force during peacetime, Fort Crockett's advantageous locale on the Gulf allowed it to become an army recreational center where vacationing military families could soak up the island ambience. Later, the primary facilities became a home for fisheries research for the U.S. Fish and Wildlife Service—and those old bunkers, I have to assume, came to house creatures that slither along their bellies. Today, the remaining buildings of the primary fort are managed by the U.S. NOAA National Marine Fisheries Service. Some of the structures house parts of Texas A&M-Galveston, while others host the Texas Institute of Oceanography. The San Luis was built in 1984, and according to a hotel manager I spoke, to the original plan for the resort called for imploding the bunkers and making the grounds even with the Seawall. However, the engineers quickly discovered that those bunkers were just too strong, the ramparts too thick for such a plan so they were incorporated into the design.

Next time you visit Galveston and drive down Sewall, look for those old bunkers at the San Luis. Imagine the large guns as a sentinel toward the Gulf protecting the state's coast from submarines. But be careful if you walk barefoot around the hotel grounds—some of those snakes could still be there!

Keeping the Enemy in Texas: World War II POW Camps

FOR MY AND SOME PREVIOUS GENERATIONS, when anyone mentions "prisoner of war" we no doubt mentally picture a crude jungle enclosure manned by Asian captors with menacing rifles and bamboo palisades. Such is the influence of popular culture (Chuck Norris and the "Missing in Action" films), and the pervasiveness of the images from the Vietnam era. But all wars produce prisoners requiring POWs to be housed in some way, and American entry into World War II brought a new phenomenon to the United States—foreign prisoners on American soil.

The Japanese bombing of Pearl Harbor thrust the U.S. into what had been largely a European war, a conflict that the nation was not fully prepared to wage. As the nation's armed forces went into battle another realization soon hit the nation's military planners and political leaders: what were we to do with prisoners? Like the war effort itself, the nation was ill-prepared for the influx of huge numbers of enemy combatants. Building and maintaining large and expansive POW camps overseas would have been impractical for an army that had to be on the move chewing up territory, so the only real alternative was to ship prisoners back to American soil. Through the first part of 1945, U.S. forces averaged sending more than 40,000 POWs a month to the United States.

Partly because it is a big place and partly because of its temperate climate, but more so because of the many Texans in influential positions in Congress (military installations were big business), Texas had twice as many POW camps than any other state; at its height in 1933 Texas claimed more than thirty-three POW facilities. Most of the prisoners were German, but Italian POWs were also housed in Texas. The camps closely resembled any ordinary military installation with barracks covered by tar paper or sheet iron where the prisoners slept dormitory-style on rows of cots. They ate in a communal mess hall, and had a large yard for recreation and gathering in groups. However, there was one significant difference—the POW camps were watched by armed snipers in watchtowers and surrounded with high razor wire, often with dog patrols around the perimeter.

Some enlisted POWs were required to work outside the camp, usually in agricultural activities, but also in factories. Most of these prisoners were housed in "branch camps" in numbers less than a hundred. Texas farmers, hit hard by the labor shortage of war time, eagerly paid the federal government the prevailing wage of $1.50 per day for POW labor. Prisoners received canteen coupons for their work. German POWs also worked in public work projects in Texas. They helped to build Denison Dam, which stored the waters of Lake Texoma on the Red River, state road projects, and they also served in orderly capacities at Harmon General Hospital in Longview.

For the most part, relations between the prisoners and home-front Texans were good, even cordial. Many people fondly recalled their interactions with the prisoners who worked on local farms, and prisoner accounts generally mention the fair and even treatment they received from both their military captors and the local folk. Amiable feelings among the majority did not mean that all accepted their condition, and some POWs made attempts to escape. Twenty-one POWs did escape from their enclosures, but none even made it out of the state. Most of the escapees wandered away from their work details and authorities found them fairly quickly. Some did fashion elaborate plots. One escapee from the Hearne facility (the largest in Texas) constructed a raft and thought he could float down the Brazos to the sea and eventual freedom back in Germany; another from the Mexia camp struck out across the countryside, but did not get far before a very angry Brahman bull "treed" the hapless prisoner, who became very grateful upon his rescue.

At the war's end the army decommissioned the camps. They sold some of the buildings off at public auction, while other facilities, such as the camp at Huntsville, became parts of colleges and schools. Buildings and land at Camp Swift near Bastrop today constitute part of a University of Texas cancer research center. Years later some German POWs, remembering their time at Texas POW camps, actually moved to Texas and became residents. POWs and prisoner camps in Texas, all were a part of an important, and very unique, chapter in our state's history.

Ahead of Its Time: The Shamrock Hotel

ANYONE WHO HAS VISITED HOUSTON certainly knows that the Bayou City has its share of first-class hotels—large convention hostelries that offer luxury appointments, top-flight meeting facilities, and gracious hospitality. Many people take it for granted that all large cities have such venues, and these days I suppose most do. But that was not always the case with Texas' largest city, and the hotel that set the mold for all that came after it was the magnificent Shamrock Hotel—an enterprise conceived by an iconoclast oilman and one that was most decidedly ahead of its time.

Glenn H. McCarthy was one of the most flamboyant oil wildcatters in an era and state that was full of such men. Born in Beaumont, McCarthy left one college (Tulane) after a football injury, was expelled from another (Texas A&M) for inappropriate behavior, and dropped out of another (Rice Institute) to start a business. Eventually, he used the last penny he had to drill a successful oil well near Trinity Bay, a strike that led him to many other successful ventures and earned him the nickname "King of the Wildcatters."

McCarthy was not immune to financial risk; as an independent oilman in Texas that is often an "occupational hazard." One of those risks became the Shamrock. Completed in 1949 at a cost of $21 million (which would be the equivalent to well over $200 million in today's dollars), McCarthy envisioned his grand hotel as just the first part of what current developers would call a "multi-use venue." The Shamrock sat out in what was then the flat, rural, plain outside the city, right in the middle of what is now the Texas Medical Center. McCarthy's visionary plans included a huge shopping complex, an entertainment outlet, and smaller office buildings; at the center of it all would be the hotel, which would cater to the business and convention trade.

The Shamrock Hotel was truly a grand affair. Famed architect Wyatt C. Hedrick designed it with eighteen stories and over 1,000 rooms. It also included an elaborately landscaped garden, the largest outdoor pool in the world (it was big enough to hold water skiing exhibitions!), and a 25,000 square foot exhibition hall. The hotel opened on St. Patrick's Day 1949, and McCarthy brought in Hollywood stars and journalists from all over the globe. He also invited the entire city, which turned the occasion into a rowdy affair that caused the cancellation of a scheduled live radio broadcast. Of course, such a party was only fitting for a hotel conceived by a man who had his own label of bourbon.

The Shamrock Hotel became "the" center of Houston social activity—it even hosted its own network radio program on the ABC network. Celebrities performed in its Emerald Room nightclub, it became the scene of numerous society weddings and receptions, and the guest rooms were some of the most elaborately furnished in the world. Edna Ferber, in her classic novel *Giant*, modeled her "Conquistador Hotel" on the Shamrock—and Jett Rink was based on McCarthy.

The Shamrock was assuredly famous, but what it was not was profitable. Glamorous stars and resort amenities are nice, but a hotel as large as the Shamrock depended on paying guests and it just did not have enough. Houston business icon Jesse H. Jones had warned McCarthy that he would not be able to convince business travelers to stay at a hotel so far from downtown, advice that proved prescient. McCarthy had highly leveraged his assets to build his palace and his cash reserves took a huge hit, which forced him to take on more debt in an endless cycle to try and make his dream a reality. He never built the elaborate shopping complex he had planned, and the other buildings and businesses also never materialized. Finally, McCarthy defaulted on a loan in 1952 and the Equitable Life Assurance Company took possession of the Shamrock.

Eventually, the Hilton Hotel Corporation acquired and operated the hotel as the Shamrock Hilton until 1986, when the oil bust finally squeezed the life out of the old grand place. Hilton essentially gave the Shamrock to the Texas Medical Center, and in turn it was demolished and turned into a parking lot. McCarthy recovered and went on to make another large pile of money. His original vision of a large, fashionable, iconic shopping center influenced the building of The Galleria in the early 1970s. Today, Houston is chock full of convention hotels and its George Brown Convention Center hosts everything from automobile shows, an oil well exposition, to political conventions. So maybe Glenn McCarthy's Shamrock was not a "white elephant"—instead, it was just a little before its time.

A Resting Place Fit for Texans: The Texas State Cemetery

WHENEVER I TRAVEL TO AUSTIN I try to make a stop at the Texas State Cemetery, a bucolic piece of ground between Navasota and Comal streets just east of the Capitol. It is a well-maintained and peaceful garden that serves as the final resting place for governors, senators, state heroes, and iconic figures such as Albert Sidney Johnston, Stephen F. Austin, J. Frank Dobie, and Ben McCulloch. It is a memorial befitting such a state, but that was not always so; only a restoration process in the 1990s made it the grand setting that it is today.

The first time I ever visited the cemetery I was lost—literally, lost. Austin confused me in 1993 (it still does) and somehow I ventured under I-35 into a part of the city that I had never seen. After traveling a block or two I saw a something rarely observed in an urban setting—a neglected, rural-looking cemetery that had obviously seen its better days. I was more shocked when I read the small sign on the fence surrounding the plot: "Texas State Cemetery." Surely this was not *the* Texas State Cemetery, the burial place of Stephen F. Austin? This place was shabby and unkempt—as a Texan I was disgusted and angry.

How did it get in such a state? After all, it began as a noble endeavor from a state proud of its past. When Texas hero Edward Burleson died in 1851, the Texas legislature established the state cemetery in East Austin for the purpose of honoring state officials upon their burial. But other than the odd placement here and there after its beginnings the site was largely ignored (primarily due to a lack of funding). The thought of a state cemetery revived with the burial of Civil War dead in plots on the grounds, and eventually, it became the primary burial grounds for Texas' Civil War veterans.

Interest lagged once more until the turn of the twentieth century when a revival in honoring Texas' revolutionary and Republic past began. Stephen F. Austin was moved from his burial place in San Felipe to the State Cemetery in 1910. The Texas Senate passed a bill calling for prominent Texans to be buried at the site in 1927. Before the project ended more than 70 notable Texans were either buried or reinterred at the site. The legislature codified the requirements for burial in the cemetery in 1953. According to the statute, plots were restricted to those who meet the following requirements: member or ex-member of the legislature, Confederate veteran, elected state official, an appointed state official, or an individual designated by governor's proclamation or a resolution of the Legislature, and the spouse of anyone meeting such criteria. But despite such interest, as the 1950s ended the state once more seemingly forgot about its official cemetery; monetary support lagged and tourists, visitors, and officials alike forgot about the plot, which led to the deplorable condition I found it in during the early 1990s.

Fortunately, I was not the only one who thought the cemetery an embarrassment. Then Lieutenant Governor Bob Bullock shared my anger at the condition of the cemetery, and he was in a position to take action. He organized and coaxed the legislature to fund a full-scale renovation of the grounds. The grave markers were cleaned, the grounds landscaped and manicured, and trees, shrubbery, and other plant life became features of the cemetery. The project constructed a new visitor's center, a plaza, and a beautiful memorial wall. Rededicated in March 1997, the newly restored Texas State Cemetery was now a memorial ground fit for the heroes and icons of the Lone Star State.

Today visitors to the Texas State Cemetery are greeted by a well-maintained, modern tourist attraction. Guides and maps readily direct you to the graves along manicured walkways and soaring memorials. If you visit Austin make sure you take a trip to see this impressive feature, but do not forget that it was once almost a forgotten treasure.

III: Events

The Ill-Fated Matamoros Expedition

TEXANS STILL REVERE THE TEXAS REVOLUTION, and many consider it the most significant event in the state's history. The Battle of the Alamo is well-chronicled, a chapter that has been shared through the ages, but many other seminal events in that fight remain much less well known. This column recently examined the Siege of Bexar, and in the next few weeks will continue to explore some of these lesser-known events.

After the initial fight of the war at Gonzales, and the Texian rebel capture of San Antonio, the situation in Texas began to descend into chaos. The Texians did not seem to have a concrete idea of what they hoped to accomplish with their revolt. Some leaders, such as Sam Houston, pressed for a declaration of independence, while others, like James Miller of Nacogdoches and a wavering Stephen F. Austin, hoped to work out an agreement of conciliation within the Mexican federal apparatus. Partisanship, personal enmity, and others who saw profit in rebellion all contributed to confusing the situation on the ground in Texas.

Texian forces had seized all the potential military strongholds in Texas by early 1836. San Antonio was in the hands of the victorious troops who had defeated Martin Perfecto Cos`, a detachment of men held the presidio at Goliad, and the Mexican army had abandoned Nacogdoches as early as 1832. Many of the soldiers in the field, as well as some military leaders began to believe that the fighting in Texas was over and the time was now ripe either to take the fight into the interior of the country, or to leave the field, return to their families, and allow the political process to begin. Political meetings contributed to the confusion as they bickered over the direction of the conflict. The Texian army, as well as the populace, began to disintegrate into factional camps that lacked cohesion.

After the end of the Siege of Bexar, many of the remaining troops in San Antonio stripped the city of its supplies and traveled to Goliad, where they hoped to join a scheme developed by James Grant, a Scottish physician who had some dubious claims on lands near Matamoros, and who some also suspected of being a British agent bent on separating Mexico's northern frontier so he could establish a British client-state. James Bowie and some volunteers under his command were part of this faction. Grant's scheme centered on invading Matamoros, taking the key city on the Rio Grande, and then fomenting rebellion in the surrounding region. A successful rebellion against Santa Anna would also restore him to political power that would allow him to perfect his land claims. Grant had also convinced Francis Johnson and James W. Fannin, who were commanding a group of volunteers mostly from the United State that had just arrived on the coast, to join him on his filibuster.

Sam Houston realized the folly of competing factions to the overall success of the Revolution, and he also knew that Santa Anna would not allow the Texian actions to stand and would raise and march a large army to deal with Texas. In order to defeat Santa Anna Texans would have to be united, but he was largely powerless to stop such independent excursions. The Consultation that had met in November 1835 had made Houston the commander of the Texian Army, but it prohibited him from exercising command over any volunteers or "troops already in the field." Essentially, Houston was a general with nothing to lead as he could not issue any binding orders to the troops gathered at Goliad and itching to march to Matamoros. Still, he knew that he had to try and at least stop the invasion, so he traveled to Goliad and delivered an impassioned speech advising the men not to follow Johnson, Grant, and Fannin to Matamoros.

Houston managed to convince some of the men to leave the expedition, most notably James Bowie. Houston asked Bowie to take his men back to San Antonio, gather the few remaining troops in the city, destroy the Alamo, and retreat to the north and east and await instructions from him. The problem with this was that it was a request as Houston could not order Bowie to take such action. As we know, when Bowie arrived in San Antonio he formulated a different plan of action.

Upon arriving in Goliad, Johnson and his men joined Grant, but

Fannin—beginning a pattern that would become regular for him—was indecisive. Eventually, Fannin opted out of the Matamoros Expedition in favor of fortifying and defending the presidio at La Bahia, which he called Fort Defiance. Houston also advised Fannin to abandon La Bahia and march north, advice that he did not take and would come to, no doubt, regret. With Fannin out of the plan, Johnson and Grant continued toward first San Patricio eventually to march to Matamoros with approximately 200 men. When they reached San Patricio, Johnson paused to gather supplies and more troops, while Grant and approximately 25 troops marched to camp and wait on Agua Dulce Creek.

Santa Anna had indeed raised an army and was marching to Texas. When the Mexican president reached the Rio Grande he sent one contingent of his troops to sweep through south Texas—specifically to march to Goliad and take back the La Bahia presidio—under the very able command of Jose Urrea. Urrea was perhaps the best trained of Santa Anna's commanding officers, and he brought with him men of the Mexican cavalry, highly skilled horsemen well-suited for combat on the South Texas plains. Johnson and Grant were headed for a direct collision with Urrea.

The collision first happened at San Patricio. Urrea's troops arrived early in the morning of February 27, 1836 and surrounded the town, catching the Texians by surprise. As the sun came up, he thoroughly routed the inexperienced band with adroit precision. Johnson actually escaped and made his way back to Refugio. The Texians not killed in the battle were rounded up and imprisoned in Matamoros.

Urrea next backtracked to Agua Dulce and brutally surprised and defeated Grant's small group on March 2. The Matamoros Expedition was over before it even started, and it was also the signal of a new reality in the Texas Revolution. At the same time, of course, Santa Anna's main force had the Alamo under siege and would soon storm the old mission and put its soldiers to the sword. Urrea was now pointed toward Fanning and his troops at La Bahia, another battle that would not turn out well for the Texians.

Miscalculation and Bravery: The Battle of Coleto

THE PREVIOUS ENTRY EXAMINED the foolhardy Matamoros Expedition, a disastrous outcome that would have a direct influence on the next episode of the Texas Revolution, the Battle of Coleto, which was the precursor to the infamous Goliad Massacre. James W. Fannin, the commander of the Texian forces at Goliad, made a series of mistakes and miscalculations that led to the battle and then executions that inspired the defiant "Remember Goliad" cry at the Battle of San Jacinto. History has not treated Fannin well, justifiable in many ways, but his foolishness should not detract from the courage he showed in battle and in facing Santa Anna's ordered execution.

After Fannin received word of the fate of Francis Johnson and James Grant's failed Matamoros campaign, the former West Point cadet had a decision to make: stay and try to defend La Bahia Presidio from Mexican advance, a decision that had little chance of success, or take Sam Houston's advice, abandon Goliad, and fall back to the north to merge with Houston's troops and fight the Mexican army in East Texas. Fannin's potential actions became more complicated when he received word from William B. Travis begging for relief at the Alamo. Fannin delayed making any decision, and instead send 150 of his men to Refugio to reconnoiter the movements of General Jose Urrea's army after it had defeated the men bound for Matamoros.

The dispatch of men to Refugio cost Fannin valuable time and forces. Fannin refused to either move toward the Alamo—which would have been the worst decision he could make since his presence would not have helped save the isolated garrison—or leave his South Texas fort to join Houston. Urrea met and defeated Fannin's detachment at Refugio under the command of Amos King on March 15 after a three-day battle, and in the process he captured communications from Fannin, which meant he knew what Fannin had planned and how to proceed.

Fannin finally ordered the evacuation of La Bahia late in the afternoon on March 18, but it did not begin until mid-morning March 19, another waste of valuable time. Furthermore, he made the curious decision to take along artillery pieces ill-suited for a march—and ones that would have been useless to Urrea's troops who were moving predominantly as a light-cavalry unit—and far too many muskets than he had men. To make matters worse, he had the men pack provisions for only a few days march. Progress out of Goliad was slow as rivers and poor transport equipment slowed their leave.

General Urrea had expected to lay siege to the presidio, but he learned of Fannin's departure within a few hours of the Texian action. He quickly mobilized his forces and set out in pursuit of the retreating Texian army. Urrea seemed to understand what Fannin did not; if he could catch the Texians on the open plains he had the advantage, but if they reached the cover of Coleto Creek or another river bed and foliage, then that benefit dissipated. He left his artillery and at least half his forces at Goliad and quickly moved to catch up to Fannin's troops.

Fannin and the Texians were running out of time. He had paused the troops at mid-afternoon to fix a broken cart, even while just a march of no more than an hour would have allowed him to reach the protection of Coleto Creek. He then had the main troop pause longer while he sent scouts to reconnoiter the woodlands surrounding the creek's banks. The delay cost Fannin dearly as no more than thirty minutes after he ordered the scout patrol out, Urrea's advance cavalry unit arrived and engaged the Texians.

Fannin may have made mistakes that cost his command time and advantage, but his abbreviated West Point education had taught him tactics. He quickly organized his men into a square perimeter and tried to make it to higher, better defensible ground before Urrea's main detachment reached the area, but he had little ammunition, dwindling provisions, and no way to counter Urrea's highly trained and effective cavalry. While he probably knew the best he could do was to make a stand and ask for terms, Fannin arrayed his troops into an effective three-deep hollow square and prepared to defend their position.

Urrea and the remainder of his men reached Fannin's position later in the afternoon and attacked Fannin with approximately five hundred men. The battle raged until after sunset, and the Texian's held their position even under three direct Mexican charges. But despite their bravery, the Texian situation had hardly changed; they were still surrounded, still low on supplies, and had now suffered a number of casualties—including Fannin who had been shot through the arm. Dawn brought a greater revelation; Urrea had brought up more troops from Goliad and some artillery. Fannin knew resistance was futile so he sent word to Urrea for surrender terms. Urrea replied that surrender would be unconditional, but there seemed to be an implication that the prisoners would be treated fairly. Fannin turned his sword over to the Mexican commander and his men marched back to Goliad as prisoners.

Later accounts seem to imply that Urrea did intend to hold the Texians under guard and eventually parole them to the United States. That certainly may be true, but Urrea was an officer in the Mexican army and his commander was Santa Anna, and the Mexican president had declared that all traitors to the Mexican nation—and let's be honest, the Texians were traitors—would be put to the sword. Santa Anna ordered Urrea to execute the prisoners, so on Palm Sunday, March 27, 1836, the Mexican jailers marched them out of the presidio and then shot them at the Goliad Masscare. James W. Fannin, who was convalescing and not marched out, was shot in the face shortly after his men. Some men, including Herman Erhenberg whose later accounts provided posterity with the greatest detail of the massacre, escaped the slaughter and told the fateful tale. Thus the famous rally-cry at the Battle of San Jacinto, "Remember the Alamo! Remember Goliad!"

Sam and Santa Anna: The Day They Met

TWO FIGURES DOMINATED TEXAS' HISTORY in the days of the Texas Revolution: Sam Houston on the Texian side, and Jose Antonio de Padua Marìa Severino Lòpez de Santa Anna, the Mexican president and commander of the Mexican forces in Texas. As far as anyone knows, and there is no reason to think differently, the two men had never met until the early afternoon of April 22, 1836 when Texian soldiers brought General Santa Anna, clad in a private's uniform, to Sam Houston as he lay, in pain from shattered ankle suffered in battle the day before, under an large oak tree near the San Jacinto battleground. If accounts and legends are accurate, The Mexican President said to the victorious Houston, "You have captured the Napoleon of the West." I have my doubts as to whether or not Santa Anna said such a thing, but it makes for a good story.

The Battle of San Jacinto was one of the most lopsided and decisive in military history. The actual "battle" portion lasted but eighteen minutes, and the Texians wholly routed the surprised Mexican troops. Houston ordered his troops to advance across the prairie at about 4 o'clock that April 21 afternoon, and the Texians caught the Mexican forces unaware. The Texian casualties were light, with eleven killed and thirty wounded. One of those was Sam Houston when, as he led a charge atop his horse Saracen, a musket ball shattered his ankle. Houston was taken from the field and placed under an oak tree, where he was also given doses of opium to help with his pain.

While the battle was over in eighteen minutes, the slaughter and killing continued for hours. Texians, enraged by the perceived atrocities committed by Mexican troops at the Alamo and Goliad, indiscriminately killed Mexican soldiers, many trying to surrender. Houston feared that Mexican reinforcements were on the way, and that his army must reorder and prepare for a counter-attack, so he ordered his officers to make such attempts, but they had little luck as the Texians that day were more interested in blood-lust than military decorum. At one point Houston, delirious from pain and opium, saw what he thought was a group of Mexican soldiers advancing toward his spot. He cried, "All is lost! All is lost," as he believed the counter-attack had occurred and the Mexicans were in charge of the field. However, the advancing column was not a Mexican force, but instead a group of Mexican prisoners taken by troops under Houston's fellow Nacogdoches resident Thomas J. Rusk, being marched to an improvised POW area near the general's tree.

One person the Texians were intent on capturing was Santa Anna, but he was no where to be found. If accounts are accurate—and there is some dispute since many of the Mexican chronicles of the battle came well after the fight and were recorded by Santa Anna's political enemies—when the fighting began Santa Anna emerged from his tent confused and in a drug-induced stupor; the Mexican general was a habitual opium user. The "Napoleon of the West" either ordered a Mexican private to give him his uniform, or he took one from a dead soldier, but however he obtained it, Santa Anna left his uniform near his tent and retreated into the reeds near Vince's Bayou adjacent to the battlefield.

Santa Anna spent the entire night of April 21 hiding in the tall grass near the bayou, somehow avoiding Texian patrols and other operations in the field. As morning dawned the next day, Sam Houston ordered a search of the surrounding area to round up any Mexican soldiers who may have escaped. Shortly before noon, on April 22, Sergeant J.A. Sylvester, and his men Joel Robinson, Joseph Vermillion, Alfred Miles, and David Cole found what they thought was a Mexican private on his hands and knees and covered in mud crouching in the reeds. They apprehended him and took him back toward the Texian camp.

Sergeant Sylvester had no idea that he had captured Santa Anna, and the Mexican General may have continued to dodge discovery if not for what happened when they got back to the camp. Again, there are two stories about how the Texians ascertained that they had Santa Anna in custody. The most accepted version is that as Santa Anna was being brought toward the area that housed the Mexican prisoners the men inside the area began to shout, "El Presidente! El Presidente! Thus, the ruse was up for Santa Anna. Another one, and I like this one better, is that all prisoners were ordered to strip before they entered the compound to make sure they were not carrying any concealed weapons. Santa Anna had "borrowed" a private's uniform, but in his haste he had forgotten to discard his monogrammed silk underpants. Thus, his identity was literally written on his underwear.

However his identity was exposed, Santa Anna was immediately taken to Houston. Awakened from a nap, Houston greeted Santa Anna warmly, but it was a tense situation. Most of the Texian soldiers wanted the Mexican President immediately executed, but Houston spared his life as he realized he was worth much more alive than dead. The two men chatted with the aid of a translator, and then Houston had Santa Anna write an order to General Vincente Filisola, the commander of the Mexican troops marching toward East Texas, telling him to retreat back to Mexico. Surprisingly, Filisola complied. Santa Anna was eventually whisked away to Velasco, where he was imprisoned on a ship moored off the coast. The two men, so instrumental in shaping of the history of Texas, never met again. Santa Anna was eventually paroled and sent to the United States, while Houston went to New Orleans to receive medical treatment and recover from his wound. He would of course, go on to serve as the president of the Republic of Texas twice, and senator and governor from the state. Santa Anna? He was not done either, and he would eventually recapture the presidency of Mexico—five more times!

Not Our Finest Hour: The Cherokee War of 1839

EAST TEXAS IS AN ALMOST PERFECT "borderland," a region where Indians, Spaniards, the French, Mexicans, and Americans all collided. Such overlaps quite often caused tension as squabbles over land titles and dominion led to violence. Our past is full of examples, but some of the most poignant of those battles pitted European and American settlers against Native Americans. The Spanish and Mexicans fought with Tawakonis, Caddo, Waco, and other peoples in the region through the years, battles that hastened poor relations and feelings of enmity, although it was a lack of immunity from European diseases that caused most of these tribes to diminish in numbers and eventually cease to be a real presence in the region. After those two groups ceased to have control over the region, American settlers continued the pattern of conflict and battle with Indian peoples.

When other Native peoples diminished in East Texas still more moved in to take their place. One such tribe were the Coushatta's and their kin the Alabama. Another late arrival was a band of Cherokees under the leadership of Duwali. Also known as Bowl, Duwali was born in North Carolina in 1756, but both internal and external pressures led him to move his people first to Missouri, then to Arkansas, and finally to just north of Nacogdoches. Duwali was well known to the white settlers of the region as he negotiated a land grant with Spanish authorities in the 1822, cooperated with the Mexican civil authorities to end the nascent Fredonian Rebellion in 1827, and was a frequent visitor to Nacogdoches. The Texas Cherokee's troubles began when they got in the middle of the fight between Americans and Mexico over Texas.

Duwali wanted to secure full, legal title to land between the Angelina, Neches, and Trinity Rivers, and moved to treat with the Mexican government for such an agreement in 1833. Mexico was willing to listen, but because the Cherokee band had cooperated with the American settlers in the region in the past they were skeptical about Duwali's loyalty. Given such mistrust, negotiations broke down between the two parties, which left the Cherokee in a precarious position. Still committed to securing proper title, Duwali, Sam Houston, and John Forbes all agreed on a treaty between the Cherokee and Texas' provisional government in February 1836 to grant the Cherokee possession of the lands between the Angelina and Sabine Rivers northwest of the Old San Antonio Road. In exchange, Duwali promised to stay out of the brewing fight between Mexico and the Texians.

Texas, of course, won that fight and moved to set up a permanent government. Although Duwali thought he had an agreement, the treaty still had to be approved by the new Texas government. The new government, full of new arrivals and others intent on exploiting as much of Texas' lands as possible certainly did not want a huge chunk of territory in Cherokee hands. Thus, they declared all provisions of the treaty null and void in December 1837.

As the first elected Texas president, Sam Houston was able to keep a lid on much of the tension between Texas and the Cherokee, although Thomas J. Rusk would use the cover of the so-called Cordova Rebellion to unsuccessfully try and extricate the Cherokee from East Texas. Houston's term ended in December 1838, and his successor, Mirabeau B. Lamar, was not inclined to try a peaceful solution to what many called the "Indian Problem."

Once again using a dubious pretext, a letter captured from Manuel Flores that seemed to suggest an alliance between Mexico and Indians to take back Texas, Lamar ordered the Texas Army in July 1839 to expel Duwali and the Cherokee. Under the command of Edward Burleson and Thomas J. Rusk, five hundred Texas troops took the field to move the Cherokee out of Texas and into Arkansas. Duwali understood that resistance was fruitless, but the Cherokee had planted crops—staples that they would need the profits from if they were to pull up stakes and move. Duwali was willing to move, but resisted signing an agreement if they could not harvest and if they were to have an armed escort.

When the sides could not agree, the Texan forces attacked the Cherokee village and began what is known as the Battle of the Neches, fought near that river just west of present-day Tyler. After a few hours of battle Duwali and his band retreated, but the Texans chased after them the next day. The two sides fought a small skirmish near the headwaters of the Neches on July 17, but the Cherokee forces had to flee once again when the main Texas army arrived in the middle of the fight. Duwali, alone in the field after the retreat as his age prevented him from moving quickly (he was 83), was killed by Texas troops even though he offered no resistance to capture. The Texas Army chased the Cherokee to near present-day Grand Saline where a final fight further thinned their numbers. Beaten and bloodied, the Cherokee retreated to the Indian Territory (Oklahoma). Their days in Texas were over.

Lowering The Lone Star

I DO NOT THINK THAT I HAVE EVER met a Texan who was not ready to brag about our state, be it size, economy, people, or football teams. But of all the things that Texans love to brag about, it is our history that seems to inspire the most passion and—yes—braggadocio. Texans tend to think that we have a unique history, and while in some ways we do, it is probably not as unique as we would like to think. However, when anyone makes a statement like I just did suggesting that Texas is, perhaps, not unique, almost any Texan worth his salt will respond (usually quite loudly) that one of our most exclusive attributes is that we were once an independent nation and no other state ever was. Actually, that is not altogether correct since California spent almost a month as an independent republic, and we always seem to forget or overlook the Kingdom of Hawaii. So, we are not the "only one."

That said, Texas did spend the most time as an independent nation. The Republic of Texas existed for more than nine full years, and was recognized as such by many of the most powerful nations in the world. But it was one born in chaos and disarray, a condition it never really overcame. It was never meant to be permanent, and one just biding its time until inclusion in the Union occurred. It would be a long, lonely nine years before it could become a part of the nation that many Texans had left behind.

When Texas won its independence from Mexico after the Battle of San Jacinto, it quickly held an election to elect a legitimate government. Held in October 1836, the election made Sam Houston the first elected president of Texas, and seated the Texas Congress. The balloting also included a plebiscite that asked Texans to cast a vote as to what they preferred: to remain independent or become a part of the United States. By an overwhelming margin, Texans expressed their partiality for becoming a part of the U.S.

The adjoining of Texas to the United States seemed, on the surface, an easy task. After all, U.S. President Andrew Jackson, the most powerful and influential man in America, favored the annexation, the potent southern congressional delegation was fervently for adding Texas, and the zeal of Manifest Destiny suggested a majority of Americans itched to expand the country westward. What people did not see was how passionate—and divisive—the slavery issue had grown in the U.S. since the 1820s. Slavery as a political issue had not overtly reared its head in American politics since the Missouri Compromise in 1821, but in the interim since that date the institution had become so entrenched in the American South that it was no longer just an institution vital to the southern economy, but had been embedded and intertwined into the social and cultural milieu of the region. By the 1830s, the most dominant theme in southern life was the protection of slavery and plantation agriculture.

Thus for southerners, Texas was the manifestation of the extension of the slavocracy. But conversely, for northerners expansion of slavery meant an increase in the power of the South and its influence on the power and politics of the nation. That meant that there was a rising movement in the North to keep slavery confined to its current borders, which necessitated opposing the annexation of Texas. Texas became a political battle, which meant that Jackson, along with his successor Martin Van Buren, could not make annexation a reality. Texas would have to strike out on its own.

It became a very rough road. Houston's first term was beset with financial difficulties, Indian threats, and the specter of a reinvasion by Mexico. Mirabeau Lamar's presidency made the question of annexation moot since he saw Texas as a developing empire that would rival and even eclipse the U.S. When Houston took office for his second stint as president in 1841, while he still favored annexation conditions—specifically the slavery question—still made the U.S. keep Texas at arm's length.

Houston did have a card to play, one that would once again pique American interest in Texas. European powers France and Great Britain—particularly the British—wanted to have access to Texas' markets as well as make sure that Texas survived to check American expansion across the continent. Houston understood this and began to dally with the British, even suggesting that British support for the nation would ensure that British aims were always considered. The Texas president knew that the U.S. would respond, and by 1844 Texas once again became an issue.

During the election of 1844, Tennessee's favorite son James Knox Polk unexpectedly gained the Democratic Party's presidential nomination. He did so by basing his candidacy on American expansion, including the annexation of Texas. In the general election in November Polk handily beat the Whig standard bearer Henry Clay. It seemed that Americans were casting ballots to include Texas in their Union.

Even before Polk could take office, lame-duck John Tyler hatched a scheme to annex the Lone Star Republic. Knowing full well that an annexation treaty was an impossibility since it would require a two-thirds majority, Tyler and Democratic congressional leaders made a deal to have Texas' annexation approved by joint-resolution instead of a treaty. Once again northern congressmen rallied against the measure, but through Democratic Party loyalty and southern power, both the Senate and House approved the measure.

Now the ball was in Texas' court. Houston's term had ended and most assumed that his successor Anson Jones, a Houston supporter, would ease the resolution through the Texas Congress. But Jones began to have second thoughts about Texas giving up its independence, so he suspended the vote on the measure for ninety days so the British could try to negotiate Mexican recognition of Texas' independence and other instruments designed to keep Texas out of the U.S.

Such efforts went for naught. Texans were ready for annexation, and the people overwhelmingly supported the resolution. Jones had no choice but to acquiesce, and in July 1845, Texas approved the U.S. overture. Texas was now to become part of the U.S. Texans elected a new state government in October 1845, the U.S. Congress accepted Texas' results on December 28, and on December 29, 1845, James K. Polk signed legislation making Texas the 28th state in the Union. The Texas officials were slated to take office on February 19, 1846, and on that day Anson Jones walked to the front of the Capitol building in Austin, lowered the Lone Star Flag, and with tears streaming down his face said, "The Republic of Texas is no more."

A Vision of Ruin: Sam Houston, Texas, and Secession

WE ARE CURRENTLY IN THE MIDST of the 150th anniversary of the Civil War, a war that without a doubt, at least in my mind, was the darkest chapter in our nation's history. But was it actually necessary for the South to secede and initiate the most devastating war this nation has ever known? I am not sure if scholars, commentators, or anyone else will ever reach a satisfactory answer to such a question, but one person at the time the war began warned anyone who would listen that the coming war would be worse than anyone imagined—Texas hero Sam Houston.

When talk of secession began in the 1850s, Senator Sam Houston told the secessionists to be very careful for what they asked. During the debate over the Kansas-Nebraska Act, and the 1856 presidential campaign, southern "fireaters" had begun to speak openly of secession. Houston worried that such talk was dangerous to the Union, and that any talk of secession was dangerous and would lead the South to "ruin."

Back home in Texas the secessionists, led by firebrand Louis Wigfall, loudly proclaimed against the "Black Republicans," and wailed that Republican victories threatened to end slavery and with it the "southern way of life." Houston was faced with a dilemma: should he continue in the U.S. Senate and battle secessionist threats on a national stage, or return home and at least try to convince Texans not to commit a horrible mistake. As he so often did, Sam Houston chose to try to save Texas, and he entered the 1857 governor's race against Hardin Runnels.

Houston's ideas on secession would, to some, seem contradictory. Houston was, after all, a slave owner and he had always defended the institution to critics. But he was also, like his mentor Andrew Jackson, a nationalist who believed the protection of the Union rose above all ideology. For Sam Houston that was the constant, the one factor that took precedence over all others.

Houston campaigned throughout the state with one primary message—southern extremism, which included secession, only increased the possibility of threats from the North and would not protect the South or its institutions. Louis Wigfall followed Houston around on the campaign trail and told all who gathered that Houston was a "traitor to the South, to slavery, and to our way of life."

Sam Houston had never lost an election in his life, but the hill he had to climb in this election was just too steep; the slavery issue, combined with the perceived Republican threat and the southern idea that in order for slavery to remain alive the region must expand, made him just too convenient a target. Runnels defeated the "Hero of San Jacinto" by more than 4,000 votes.

The now sixty-five year old general may have lost an election, but he was not unbowed in his resolve. He continued to speak out against secession, at various times calling such sentiment "madness," and on another occasion imploring his fellow southerners to not make "rash decisions." In a way, Houston knew that railing against secession was a lost cause for the whole of the South, but I think that he thought he could at least save Texas from making such a poor choice. So, he threw his hat into the ring and announced his candidacy for governor in 1859.

This time Houston focused more of his campaign on local issues, such as protection of the frontier and the state's finances, than he did national questions. The strategy worked—Houston beat the incumbent Runnels by a healthy margin. But Sam Houston was taking over the governorship at a precipitous time because secessionist sentiment was growing with the Republican national electoral successes in 1858 and 1859. Texans, with most other southerners, opened the 1860 presidential election year in a "rule or ruin" mood. Southern Democrats demanded that the national party pass a plank in support of slavery; if they did not, they would leave the party and nominate their own candidate. That is exactly what happened, and with the Democrats divided Republican Abraham Lincoln won a convincing victory.

South Carolina was the first state to secede, followed quickly by Florida, Alabama, and Mississippi. Wigfall and the other "fireaters" in Texas began to call for a secession convention to follow suit, but Governor Houston refused. He said that the "price of liberty is blood, and if an attempt is made to destroy our Union there will be bloodshed to maintain them." He told anyone who listened that secession meant war, and it would be a war that the South could not win. In the end, it did little good—despite his best efforts, in February 1861, Texas voted to secede from the Union and join the newly formed Confederacy.

The new secessionist government required all officials to take a loyalty oath. Ordered to appear to take the oath at noon on March 15, 1861, Houston instead stayed in the capitol basement whittling on a piece of soft pine. Three times the secretary of the convention called his name, but the Hero of San Jacinto remained in a chair, wordless, but firm of his resolve. The convention declared the governor's office vacant, and Sam Houston was forced out of office.

The Civil War did rage on, and like he predicted the South went down in terrible ruin. Sam Houston returned to his home in Huntsville broken-hearted. He would even lose a son to the war he opposed. Houston caught pneumonia in early July 1863 and slowly withered away. He died on July 26, and his last words were recorded as "Texas…Texas…" I suppose we should have listened a bit closer to the General.

Defending the Coast: The Battle of Galveston—1862

WHEN THE CIVIL WAR BEGAN IN APRIL 1861 Texas was, of course, a part of the Confederate States of America, which they joined almost immediately upon secession. One of the most integral parts of Union strategy was a naval blockade of the Confederate coastline to keep war material out, and any money-making Confederate goods from getting to world markets. The Union would also attack and attempt to capture some key ports, such as New Orleans, in another attempt to stifle Confederate commerce and break the South's ability to wage war. New Orleans fell in May 1862, and the key Texas port of Galveston next came into the Union navy's sights.

Brigadier General Paul O. Herbert commanded the Confederate District in Texas, and he became convinced that Galveston was indefensible so he removed most of the heavy artillery from the island. The Union sent Commander William B. Renshaw, a veteran of the conquest of New Orleans and a key member of Admiral David Farragut's squadron that helped to capture New Orleans, to take Galveston. Herbert had left Colonel John J. Cook in command on the island, but with his heavy guns gone and forces depleted he could offer little defense when the Union ships sailed into the harbor. Cook appealed to Renshaw to grant him a four day truce so that he could evacuate to the mainland. Renshaw agreed and the Union ships guarded the harbor against any attempts to re-occupy the city until the Forty-Second Massachusetts Infantry arrived in December to take control of the island.

Major General John B. Magruder supplanted the ineffectual Hebert shortly after the fall of Galveston, and he immediately made plans to recapture the port. Utilizing some soldiers originally recruited for Henry Sibley's invasion of New Mexico, Magruder sent Colonel Tom Green on two river steamers outfitted with cotton bales to repel Union fire to make a naval attack. To add pressure, he sent General William Scurry with infantry, cavalry, and more than twenty pieces of cannon to attack and secure the railroad bridge to the island and then make their way ashore and capture the city.

The attack began on New Year's Day, 1863 before dawn and turned into a complete Confederate rout. Scurry's men quickly seized the city's wharves and began to make inroads. The Confederate "cotton clads" and the hail of fire from Green's men aboard the ships drove the Union navy back from its positions. Renshaw's flagship ran aground on a sand bar, and the Union commander sacrificed his life and blew up his ship rather than see it fall into Confederate hands. The Union ships that remained sailed away and left Galveston to Confederate control.

The Union was never again able to capture Galveston; they only mounted token attempts for the remainder of the war. Magruder made sure Galveston was well-fortified, and it continued to operate as a port and supply depot for Confederate Texas. It was only after the war ended with Robert E. Lee's surrender at Appomattox Courthouse that federal troops, under General Gordon Granger, once again occupied the city.

Patriots or Traitors?: German Unionists and the Battle of the Nueces

TEXAS MADE ITS DECISION TO SECEDE from the Union in February 1861 through a state-wide election. The outcome of the polling reflected the mood of the Texas electorate. Well over 45,000 Texans voted for secession and less than 15,000 cast against; 122 counties voted for secession and only 18 voted against. Of the 18 counties that voted to stay loyal to the United States, the majority of those were in a cluster around Austin often referred to as the "German Belt" because the majority of the residents in those counties were of German descent, although it also included a sizable number of people of Czech heritage. Few Germans, like most Texans, owned slaves, but unlike the majority of the white residents of Texas who fully supported slavery as a mechanism to maintain the southern concept of white superiority, the Germans not only questioned the institution but they were vehemently opposed to its concept. Thus, they saw no reason to support a movement to leave the United States in order to continue the "peculiar institution."

German migration to Texas began when it was still a part of Mexico, but it greatly accelerated after the establishment of the Republic. German migrants to Texas tended to settle on the central frontier region, in the area surrounding and between Austin and San Antonio. They operated small farms, stock operations, and engaged in merchant activities. They were also joined by immigrants from other central European regions, including a significant number of Czechs. While most of these new residents came to acquire the acres of free land that Texas offered, some left Germany, and other European nations and principalities, to escape religious and political persecution. Often referred to as "Freethinkers," this group of mostly German intellectuals moved to Texas in an attempt to establish a society that was free from governmental and institutional oppression pressure, and a chance to live as free, independent, people. A tenet among the Freethinkers was their opposition to any forms of bondage.

One of those Freethinkers who came to Texas from Prussia was Frederick "Fritz" Tegener. He established a small farm in Kerr County, and his family was one of the original inhabitants of that county's town of Comfort. Tegener became one of the leading citizens of Comfort, served as the county treasurer, as well as the owner of a gristmill, which was an important business within the fairly isolated, rural region.

When Texas began to consider secession Tegener, along with most other residents of the region, actively campaigned against the measure. When Texas did secede, and the subsequent Civil War began in April 1861, he and many other locals joined the Union Loyal League, which they called a militia organized to protect Gillespie, Kendall, Kerr, Edwards, and Kimble Counties from both Indian raids (which were actually rare) and any potential Confederate actions. The latter became more urgent when the Texas legislature, citing the secession vote, the presence of the Union Loyal League, and the refusal of many county officials in the area to take a loyalty oath to the Confederacy, to be in "open rebellion" against the Confederacy and the state. While some might think it ironic that a new nation born because an area decided to oppose the larger governmental institution would consider groups with an opposing view subversive, the Confederate government of Texas decided to crush any opposition the Union Loyal League might offer. To that end, officials ordered the Fourteenth Texas Cavalry Battalion to break up and disperse the Union Loyal League's militia.

When the Union Loyal League heard of the approach of the Confederates, a small group of them agreed on Tegener as the head of their force and decided to try to make their way to Mexico, with the intention of from there going north and joining the Union Army. On the morning of August 10, 1862, they were camped on the Nueces River in Kinney County when they were attacked by Confederate troops. The initial fighting killed 19 of the 61 German-Texans. The Germans fled across the river, leaving nine of their fellow Leaguers wounded in the camp with the hope they would receive medical aid. That did not happen. When Confederate commander C.D. McRae (who was wounded in the battle) reached the encampment he immediately ordered the wounded Germans shot as traitors to the Confederacy.

The Confederate troops continued to fire and harass the Union Loyal Leaguers as they made their way toward the border. In two different skirmishes, eight more Germans fell. Tegener was seriously wounded in these later encounters, but he and what was left of his militia did make it to Mexico. Some of the Leaguers did make it north and joined the Union Army, but most reports have Tegener remaining in Mexico and working as either a miner or a farm laborer until the Civil War ended. After the war he returned to Kerr County, served in the Texas legislature, and eventually became a judge in Austin.

The Battle of the Nueces remains a source of controversy. Confederates of the time and supporters of the cause afterward have always maintained that the rebel troops who engaged the Germans at the Nueces were wholly justified in their actions and that the fight was a strategic military incident. The Union Loyal League and their defenders conversely argue that the attack was unprovoked, unnecessary, and to prove their point they usually label it as a massacre. After the war the remains of those killed that battle were returned to Comfort and buried. Today a monument in that town honors their sacrifice.

Leaving Texas: The Exodus of 1879

HISTORIAN JAMES SMALLWOOD DESCRIBED the African American experience during Reconstruction in Texas as a "time of hope and a time of despair." It was an apt description. The beginning of Reconstruction brought great hope and expectation that freedom finally meant people of African descent could enjoy the full rights of citizenship, and property rights free of oppression and prejudice. Such great optimism directly fueled the despair when, as southern whites regained control of the levers of power, "black codes," violence, and the reappearance of the concept of white superiority crushed the expectations and dreams of African Texans. The Civil War had ended slavery, but it had not finished the South's bi-racial society and its dependence on relegating blacks to the lowest levels of a caste system.

The majority of African Texans chose to try to make some sort of accommodation within the southern system. Freedom Colonies allowed some to escape the harshest of conditions, while others struggled within the segregated way of life and did the best they could. But some decided that escape was the best solution, that Texas and the South would never change and African Americans would forever be locked in an oppressive system that did not value their contributions. Thus, they chose to leave, and for these Kansas became a preferred option.

Kansas, with its tradition as a free-state that directly rejected slavery and its connection with the martyr John Brown, became known as a "promised land" among former slaves. Kansas also had land available through the Homestead Act, which also made it an attractive option. Tens of thousands of former slaves poured into Kansas from all over the South between 1875 and 1880. They founded towns such as Nicodemus and Quindaro, all in a search for what had constantly eluded them in the South—a chance to live a life free from racial animus and with the promised inalienable rights of life, liberty, and property.

The heaviest migration from Texas came from Burleson, Grimes, Walker, Waller, and Washington counties. The end of slavery—and the hope of change—had disintegrated into the harsh life of sharecropping and tenancy, a system that locked those so engaged into an almost permanent life of peonage. For African Texans, the sharecropping, or crop lien, system was exacerbated by the lack of any political or social power or influence. When you have no voice, you can affect no change. Chastened by the lack of opportunity, these African Texans chose to stake their claims in Kansas.

Some of these "exodusters," as they came to be called, boarded trains and traveled to Kansas, but most loaded up wagons with their belongings and struck out across the prairie, all looking for the life they thought they had been promised in Texas. Estimates are that more than 12,000 African Texans left in a five year period. Many did find opportunity in Kansas: land, freedom, and the rights of citizens. But human beings are too often nefarious creatures who take advantage of their fellow man. Just as many of these exodusters became the victims of scams such as supposed railroad agents selling fake railroad tickets, to faux guides offering their services to wagon trains only to abscond with the funds and goods of travelers.

Despite the hardships, most of these migrants to Kansas stayed and made their homes in what could be a harsh land. Many prospered and became prominent landowners, but perhaps the greatest hardship borne out of the Exodus of 1879 came to white landowners in the counties with the greatest concentration of blacks. Freedman, just as they had been when they were slaves, were the primary labor in the fields, but as many left to escape the brutal conditions it left owners with a severe labor shortage. As a result, to retain labor and begin to discourage flight, these land owners had to offer better terms to share-croppers and tenants. Thus, those that stayed in Texas benefitted from the exodus as well.

White Texans of the 1880s and 1890s began to construct a myth of Reconstruction, that that period was one of great privation and hardship for them as the occupying Union soldiers took away their liberties and made it difficult for them to integrate back into the Union. The reality was quite different as Reconstruction was actually quite tame, especially when you consider that southerners had, essentially, committed treason. That myth ignores another reality, one that was much more accurate: Reconstruction did not improve the lives of former slaves, and as white southerners regained political and social ascendancy they reinstituted the same racial barriers that existed under slavery. There was one difference: African Americans had some power to "vote with their feet," and many did as they packed up and left behind oppression.

Establishing Voting Barriers: From Poll Taxes to the The All-White Primary

DURING THE DAYS OF SLAVERY, the American South intentionally created a bi-racial system, a society whose fundamental structure rested upon the precept of white superiority as a method of uniting the different white classes and cultures. If you will allow me to be brutally honest, the southern message was, "While you may be poor, landless, and powerless, at least you are not black." Slavery made it relatively easy to ingrain such an idea of African descent inferiority—after all, in the white southern mind, did not the fact that they were slaves prove subordination?

When the Civil War ended Reconstruction's primary aim was to overturn the southern subjugation of the Freedmen and find a way to integrate blacks into the larger society. As long as the United States Army occupied and oversaw the occupied South there was a shred of hope of that actually happening, but with the end of Reconstruction southern political leaders, with the full cooperation of the economic elite, began to find ways to reinvigorate the pre-war bi-racial structure—but they had to do so without the naturally organizing mechanism of slavery.

We know the ultimate result. First, came unofficial methods such as sharecropping, social pressure, and economic boycott. Ultimately, after Populism brought the potential of a political union of white and black poor farmers, southern states—including Texas—began to establish the American racial apartheid system that we came to call Jim Crow.

Jim Crow took many forms, some social, some cultural, and some economic. But its most devastating form, and quite often the most effective way to guarantee white superiority, was through political barriers. Texas, like other southern states, erected a number of different voting barriers through the late nineteenth century such as grandfather clauses, literacy tests, and most effectively the poll tax. From a high of more than 70% of all eligible African Texans voting in the late 1860s, by 1885 that participation had fallen to near 40%.

Texas had to erect such elaborate designs to limit voting due to the Fifteenth Amendment, which guaranteed the franchise to all male citizens and forbade the states to limit that freedom. For that reason, while black ballots did wane, a significant number of African Texans were able to vote. However, because most blacks were Republicans, and Texas' white voters were almost fully Democrats, their votes rarely influenced elections, except in counties that had a high number of black voters, such as Harrison. Of course, as expected, counties with a large percentage of black constituencies practiced some of the most draconian methods of suppressing the vote.

The electoral arena began to change in the 1880s and early 1890s with the rise of the agrarian protest movement. First the Farmer's Alliance and later the much larger Populist Party transformed the political landscape. These movements appealed to not only rural white Texans but also African Texans. The white Democratic power structure faced a formidable challenge: if the Populists were able to unite white and black voters, and subvert franchise impediments, then they had the potential of actually winning elections and seizing power from the Democratic hegemony. Democrats needed a new way to suppress black votes.

They found it in the name of reform. Citing the need to wring corruption out of politics and open the selection of candidates up to more of the electorate, Representative Alexander Terrell introduced and the legislature passed in 1903 a law to require and regulate primaries as a means to select candidates for office. A number of local party officials immediately interpreted the law to mean that they could bar African Americans from participating in the primaries. Because Democrats wholly controlled Texas, and Republicans had no chance of winning any state-wide elections, such a practice effectively disenfranchised a number of blacks.

The primary was an effective barrier, but it was not complete as it was still haphazardly applied. That changed in 1923 when the legislature passed a law that explicitly barred African Texans from voting in Democratic primaries. But that was too drastic a step even for the non-interventionist U.S. Supreme Court of the time, and they struck down Texas' law. However, the Court left a loophole that allowed parties to declare themselves private entities and thus determine their own membership. That is exactly what the Texas Democrats did, with the legislature's full acquiescence. Texas' blacks were, for all practical purposes, excluded from the political process.

The All White primary was the law in Texas for over twenty years, and did not disappear until the Supreme Court declared it fully illegal in 1944. While the decision did cause blacks registration to climb in the 1940s and 1950s, Texas' Democrats just went back to the tried and true barriers of the past to keep African Texans from the polls. It would not be until the Voting Rights Act of 1965, and the federal oversight of polls in Texas and the South, that the U.S. began to lessen the grip of racist voting barriers in our nation. Texas played a large role in that story.

The Camp Logan Riot of 1917

TODAY HOUSTON IS A VIBRANT, diverse, cosmopolitan city, one that I often refer to as Texas' most multi-cultural and, perhaps, most tolerant. The Bayou City is one of the most active in preserving and acknowledging the sundry influences on its heritage, as well as striving for acceptance and equality for all. Such has not always been the case. Houston is a Texas city, which means that it is predominantly southern, and thus has a dubious racial past. Perhaps no event reflects such tension better than the Camp Logan Riot of 1917, often referred to as the Houston Riot.

Houston in the early 1900s was a city fully in the grip of Jim Crow. African Americans in the city lived under the yoke of racial oppression, and almost all whites believed that protection of that bi-racial culture was the most consequential factor involved in politics, economic institutions, and society.

Ironically, although many at the time probably did not grasp such incongruity, in 1917 the United States entered World War I under the auspices of "making the world safe for democracy," all the while denying its black citizens the full principles of liberty. Texas, largely due to its hospitable climate and the power of its congressmen, became one of the primary centers for military training bases. Houston, with its modern shipping and rail transportation systems, became the location of two military training facilities, one of which was Camp Logan (the other was Ellington Field).

The U.S. Army ordered the 3rd Battalion of the all-black 24th United States Infantry to Houston in July 1917 to guard the facility during its construction. They should have known better. Southern whites, ensconced in their notions of white superiority, harbored nothing but complete disdain for any concept of African Americans in any position that resembled authority or power—which included being a soldier. The soldiers of the 24th probably expected that respect would improve when they put on the uniform of their country.

To their dismay, it did not. Resentment, even outward antipathy, began to boil between the soldiers and the residents of the city.

It all came to a head on August 23, 1917. One early afternoon, two Houston police officers arrested a 24th Battalion soldier for interfering with their arrest of a black woman. As per military custom, a provost of the post, Charles Baltimore, came downtown to inquire about the charges and the soldier. When Baltimore arrived, city police met him not with professional courtesy but with threats to jail him as well. Baltimore refused to be intimidated and the Houston police began to beat him. He ran to an unoccupied house, but was soon also arrested.

The Houston authorities released Baltimore fairly quickly, but a rumor that a white mob was coming to "round up" all the soldiers of the 24th soon reached Camp Logan. In reaction, a group of soldiers took up arms and marched into downtown Houston, first to the residential neighborhood of Brunner on the north side of Buffalo Bayou (essentially the intersection of present-day Washington Avenue and Shepherd Drive), and later in the San Felipe District. In slightly over two hours, the soldiers killed sixteen whites and wounded eleven others. Four soldiers died that night, although two of them were killed by their own men. The soldier's leader, Sergeant Henry Vida, killed himself in what was described as an act of despondency.

The army acted swiftly. After a city-wide curfew on August 24, the next day all the soldiers of the 24th were ordered to board a train for Columbus, New Mexico. Eventually, some of the soldiers agreed to testify against others, and in November the largest court-martial in U.S. military history began at Fort Sam Houston in San Antonio. One hundred and ten of the soldiers were convicted of at least one charge. The army hung nineteen of them and sixty-three received life sentences. The white officers of the 24th had charges brought against them, but were never tried. The Houston police officers, whose actions triggered the riot, faced no punishment or reprimands; no white Houston citizens faced any charges.

In Houston, when the story was told it became one that said traitorous, unpatriotic (in one account of the 1930s they were even referred to as "communists"), ungrateful black soldiers decided to riot against the dutiful white citizens of Houston. The reality, of course, was that while it would be difficult to condone the actions of the soldiers of the 24th, it was certainly clear how an oppressive social system could—almost guaranteed—that something of such a nature would take place.

A Shield Against Racism: The Founding of LULAC

ONE OF THE UNFORTUNATE LEGACIES of nineteenth century Texas was racial and ethnic discrimination. Southern whites, the predominant group to populate Texas in the early 1800s, brought with them their ideas of white superiority, the most visible symbol of which was their preference and support of slavery. The concept of white superiority survived the end of slavery and was used as a method of white social unity in the years after the Civil War, which ultimately resulted in Jim Crow laws and the concepts of institutional segregation in Texas and the South.

African Americans bore the most brutal brunt of such a social construct, but they were not the only group in the state who faced significant oppression and discrimination. Tejanos, Texans of Mexican descent, were also the subjects of significant actions under the caste system of the state, discriminatory practices that became even more widespread as Tejanos dispersed out of South Texas in larger numbers, particularly as they moved to cities in the late nineteenth and early twentieth centuries. As a result, Tejanos began to form organizations to battle oppression from the majority group in Texas, which ultimately resulted in the founding of the League of United Latin American Citizens in Corpus Christi in 1929.

Tejanos, of course, arrived in Texas years before white European/Americans began to move into the state, but by the time of the Texas Revolution their population was dwarfed by the massive influx of Americans. After the Revolution, and even more so following the Mexican War, repression towards Tejanos became more pronounced than it had been even in the days before the Revolution. However, since most Tejanos lived in South Texas, the discriminatory practices were either limited there or more isolated in other regions of the state.

Instances of discrimination, segregation, and violence increased in the late nineteenth and early twentieth centuries due to a number of factors. Tejanos began to move out of South Texas, usually as railroad or agricultural workers, and as they came into other regions of the state the racial caste system of the South that begat Jim Crow segregation began to include them along with African Americans. Also, the upheavals in Mexico, culminating in the Mexican Revolution, led a greater number of people of Mexican descent to move to the state. As a result, Tejanos were placed in separate schools—and quite often their education involuntarily ended after grades five or six—and they became subject to many of the other segregationist practices of the day. For many Tejanos this was a new experience; they had certainly been treated as inferiors before, but never on such a scale or as a total social practice.

The new occurrences of exclusion led Tejanos to begin to take action to help alleviate the problems, and a number of groups began to mobilize in the early twentieth century. They formed local *mutualistas* to combat economic oppression, as well as labor and social groups to address the practices directed toward Tejanos. A number of the leaders of these local and regional groups met at the *Congreso Mexicanista*, convened by Laredo journalist Nicasio Idar in 1911. The meeting issued a number of recommendations calling for support for greater educational opportunities, an end to economic and social discrimination, but most of all a pledge to work to together to advance the cause of full civil rights for Tejanos. They formed local "Leagues" to work toward their goals.

The success of the Leagues were mixed in their earliest years, but their success grew with the end of World War I. Mexican-Americans volunteered and served in the United States Armed Forces in percentages far greater than their population, and Tejanos formed the largest group of soldiers of Mexican descent. When these veterans returned home they joined the Leagues and began to more vociferously call for civil rights. The war, as well as new opportunities to move into the middle class, had enhanced the consciousness of their American citizenship.

John Solis and Frank Leyton, both veterans, called for a meeting in San Antonio in 1921 to discuss the state of Tejano's civil rights. The meeting led to the formation of the "Order of Sons of America." The OSoA had formed seven chapters in Texas by 1929, and combined with the earlier Leagues, *mutualistas*, and other groups a call for a new statewide organization gained momentum. The first attempt to form such a group took place in Harlingen in 1927, but the result of that meeting was not combination into a statewide organization but the formation of a new group, the Latin Americans Citizens League. Such action was a beginning, but a true statewide body had not yet taken shape.

The Latin Americans Citizens League announced the instigation of another attempt to form a statewide group by calling for a meeting in Corpus Christi in 1929. At that meeting, four of the earlier organizations merged together, the Sons of America councils of Corpus Christi and Alice, the Knights of America (a splinter group of the Sons), and the Latin American Citizens League in the Rio Grande Valley and Laredo. The members wrote a constitution, which called for work toward social, educational, and civil rights, they made English their official organization language—although they stressed the importance of bi-lingualism—and they adopted a motto, "All for one, and one for all." They also selected a "shield" as their emblem, symbolizing defense against and protection from racism. They called their new organization the "League of United Latin American Citizens."

LULAC spread quickly outside the borders of Texas, and became the leading civil rights group for Mexican Americans. They made educational disparities and discrimination their primary cause in the early years, and filed numerous lawsuits seeking equal educational protection. They joined with African American organizations in the 1950s and 1960s to combat Jim Crow, and continue today as the oldest and largest Latino civil rights organization in the United States.

Commemorating Independence: The Building of the San Jacinto Monument

TEXAS ACHIEVED ITS INDEPENDENCE FROM MEXICO on April 21, 1836 when Sam Houston's troops defeated General Santa Anna's Mexican force on a plain between the San Jacinto River and Buffalo Bayou. The Texians caught the overconfident Mexican army literally napping during the afternoon of that day, and the actual battle part of San Jacinto was swiftly over, although the indiscriminate killing and capture of Mexican soldiers continued until dusk. Santa Anna was captured the next day, trying to escape in the garb of a Private, but he was soon identified and brought before Sam Houston where he continued the arrogance that had cost him in battle when he told the Texian commander that he had "captured the Napoleon of the West."

The Battle of San Jacinto may have been fleet, but the memorialization of the battlefield was anything but rapid. As early as 1856 the Texas Veterans Association began to press the Texas legislature to provide funds to build a memorial to the men who had died as well as the battle. The legislature, in 1856, was concerned with what they thought were many more pressing matters, such as opposing the "hero of San Jacinto," Sam Houston on his stance against secession, to consider the matter of remembering the battle that brought the birth of Texas. The Civil War then interceded, and the matter of a memorial at San Jacinto faded into the mists.

Finally, after more prodding from the few remaining Texas Revolution veterans, the legislature approved funding in 1893 to purchase the land where the battle took place. The state also commissioned a survey to determine the exact boundaries of the battlefield, and then began to approach land owners to sell. After four years of wrangling and some legal proceedings, the state had bought all the land it deemed part of the battle and a new state park, the San Jacinto Battleground State Historic Site, opened in 1897.

For the next forty years the site served primarily as a gathering site for veterans of the battle, as well as those of the Civil War. It was also a frequent day-trip picnic stop for Houston families. What it didn't have was a worthy monument to the battle. That would soon change. Texas was preparing to celebrate its centennial in 1936, and the Daughters of the Texas Revolution (DRT) began to lobby the legislature to once again provide money for a grand memorial to the birthplace of Texas independence. The had a powerful ally in Jesse H. Jones, the Houston financier who headed up President Roosevelt's Reconstruction Finance Corporation and one of the most powerful Texans of his day. Jones also served as the chairman of the Texas Centennial Celebration, and he envisioned building a marker that would not only commemorate the Battle of San Jacinto but every veteran who had served during the Texas Revolution. Jones suggested a large column, with an inscription at the base, that would be worthy of Texas' self-identity as the biggest and grandest state—he wanted one that was larger than any such column in the world, even the taller than the Washington Monument.

What Jesse Jones wanted he usually got, and such turned out to be the case with the San Jacinto Monument. Secured with $1.5 million in funding from the Centennial Commission, the Texas legislature, and through Jones' contacts in Washington D.C., the United States Congress, the project broke ground in March 1936. Architect Alfred C. Finn and construction engineer Robert J. Cummins, took Jones' original idea and designed an octagonal column to be constructed of reinforced concrete with an exterior of Texas limestone. It rose to a height of just over 567 feet, which made it the tallest monument column in the world. At its top was a 200 ton 34 foot high lone star, the symbol of Texas. To keep with the theme of commemoration of not just the battle but the Texas Revolution, a museum memorializing the fight for Texas independence rested at the base of the monument. With bronze doors at the front and eight engraved panels depicting the history of Texas, the museum became the centerpiece for visitors to the monument. A 5,000 seat amphitheater behind the museum projects a continuous depiction of the famous battle.

When it opened the San Jacinto Museum of History Association operated the site under a contract with the state. The state dissolved that arrangement in 1966 when the Texas Parks and Wildlife Commission took over operation. Time and decay led to a renovation and reinforcement of the monument in 1983, and in 1990 the museum was reconfigured, renovated, and revitalized to reflect a more current interpretation of the state's history. Today, the museum offers a more inclusive and diverse presentation of Texas and the Spanish-Mexican southwest. It also contains a library and archive to aid in historical research of the battle and period. During the 1990 renovation, the Jesse H. Jones Theatre of Texas Studies opened, and it shows a multi-image production on the Battle of San Jacinto.

Today the San Jacinto Monument, along with its sister memorial the *Battleship Texas*, stand as sentinels of the past among the smokestacks, shipping yards, and assorted other structures along the busy Houston Ship Channel. In many ways it seems incongruous to see such a grand structure juxtaposed in the skyline against icons of modernity. But then again, perhaps it is fitting since what happened on that prairie in April 1836 played a huge role in Texas becoming, well, Texas.

"It was a Terrible Roar:"
The New London School Explosion

IT IS A DISTINCTIVE SMELL, OFTEN REFERRED TO as "rotten eggs," but everyone now understands that when you smell that conspicuous odor your next thought is, "there's a gas leak." It is so pervasive that the smell is almost wholly associated with natural gas, so much so that most think that is what natural gas smells like. However, that is not the case; natural gas is odorless, and until 1937 no one thought to add such a noticeable stench to the gas. The reason that we now make such an additive is because of an East Texas event that wholly changed lives and a town's fortune—The New London School Explosion on March 18, 1937.

The Depression lingered into 1937, but in pockets of East Texas, some of the economic effects were less apparent, mostly due to the discovery of the huge East Texas oilfield in 1930. That pool of petroleum helped the region avoid some of the worst problems of the Great Depression, as money from the underground reserves helped create not only needed jobs, but its tax revenues helped fill the coffers of local governments and school districts. One of those fortunate districts was New London, a town in northwest Rusk County. Increased revenue from producing wells had allowed the little town to build a new, state-of-the art steel-framed E-shaped school building. It was the pride of the surrounding region, and the focal point of the little town. Then, at approximately 3:00 p.m. on March 18, that pride of the town exploded due to a faulty gas line.

The New London School District had changed the way they received its gas in January 1937. For years, United Gas Company had delivered natural gas to heat the school and run appliances in the normal manner, but in an attempt to save money, in January the district had tapped directly into the Parade Gasoline Company's residue line, a practice known as using "green" or "wet" gas. It was a practice many homes and businesses did to save money. But in this case it cost lives because the connection was faulty and gas was escaping. It accumulated beneath the building, but because it had no smell, no one knew it was happening.

The greatest disaster in American school history came at 3:05 p.m. that March day when Lemmie R. Butler, the manual training teacher, turned on a belt sander in a room that was filled with the escaping gas. When he turned the switch the gas mixture ignited and the resulting flame went into the closed space under the building where the bulk of the gas had collected. The result was an explosion in which witnesses said sounded like a "terrible roar," and another said, "The whole school seemed to lift and the ground bounced." The roof of the school fell in and buried its victims in a tomb of glass, steel, and concrete. Residents four miles away heard the explosion and a veteran of WWI said it was unlike anything he had heard since he fought in the fields of France.

The news of the explosion rapidly spread through the town and county, and parents rushed to the site. Oilfield workers left their rigs and came to the school to dig through the rubble along with parents, bystanders, and townsfolk. Many of them dug with bare hands through steel and concrete, tearing skin from their bones in their desperate attempts to reach trapped students and teachers. Finally, some heavy equipment arrived to aid in recovery. Governor James Allred sent in Texas Rangers to help care for victims and coordinate the recovery, and teams from Shreveport, Dallas, Houston, and Nacogdoches came to see what they could do to help.

Recovery efforts lasted the better part of a day, and when all was said and done, 294 of the 540 students and teachers who remained in the building had perished; the toll could have been higher if the explosion had happened thirty minutes earlier since, as usual, the first through fourth graders had been dismissed for the day at 2:30. Recriminations from parents were quick and painful, as through their grief they looked to place blame. More than seventy lawsuits for damages were filed, although few cases came to trial, and any that did were dismissed for lack of evidence. The most important result of the disaster was the passage of the state odorization law, which required the addition of that distinct smell to natural gas. Today, a granite cenotaph marks the hallowed spot of the worst school disaster in American history.

Changing Texas Politics After the War

POLITICS HAS NEVER BEEN AN ARENA FOR THE MEEK—ask our two most recent presidents if you want proof. Texas politics has never been the exception, and during the middle of the twentieth century the state's dominant Democratic Party struggled with factionalism and division, predominantly between its conservative and liberal elements. The collective effort of World War II lessened some of the bitter in-fighting, but the end of the war once again ignited the intra-party squabble. During the 1946 governor's race, two sons of East Texas, Homer Rainey of Clarksville and Beauford Jester of Corsicana, faced off in an election that pitted the two ideologies against each other, and would also determine the course of Texas politics for the next three decades.

Homer Rainey, the man who carried the liberal banner, was a newcomer to politics. In another era, Rainey may have become someone Texans celebrated. From humble beginnings in Clarksville, Rainey excelled in a number of endeavors; he was at various times a Baptist minister, a Texas League baseball star, and president of the University of Texas. But during his tenure as University president, he became embroiled in a series of disputes with the board of regents over curriculum and the concept of academic freedom. Eventually, the regents dismissed Rainey in 1944 and he turned to politics to further his ideas and philosophy.

Beauford Jester entered politics with a more conventional pedigree. Born in Corsicana, Jester's father was the state lieutenant governor for two terms in the 1890s, and he earned a law degree from the University of Texas in 1920. Jester practiced law for a while in his home town, served on the UT board in the early 1930s, and became a Railroad Commissioner for five years. He entered the 1946 campaign as somewhat of a moderate, although his sympathies clearly rested much more with the conservative faction of the party.

Five major candidates entered the 1946 race and very early a particular pattern emerged; Homer Rainey and his "liberal" philosophy became the primary target of the other four. Rainey was castigated for supporting the continuation of the New Deal, encouraging moderation on racial issues, and contributing to the "moral decay" of Texas society. Jester tended to allow the other three major candidates—Grover Sellers, Jerry Sadler, and John Lee Smith—carry the bulk of the Rainey attacks; his strategy was to simply make a run-off with Rainey and use the natural advantage of the state's conservative voters to carry him to victory.

That is exactly what happened, although in not quite the fashion the pundits expected. As the only "liberal" candidate in the race, most expected Rainey to lead the field in the first primary, but in an upset it was Jester who captured the most votes, with Rainey second and forcing a run-off. Rainey faced the very daunting task of changing the votes of people who probably voted as much against him as for other candidates. The inevitable result was a resounding victory for Corsicana's Beauford Jester.

Jester's victory changed the direction of Texas politics. During the Great Depression and even into 1944, the state's progressive forces had effectively challenged conservative dominance. A Rainey victory in the 1946 race would have perhaps signaled a political shift in Texas away from the state's typical southern conservatism. Jester's victory entrenched such ideas within the state, forcing the liberal forces to play "catch-up" for the next twenty to thirty years. Jester would tragically die during his second term, but his even more conservative lieutenant governor, Allan Shivers, would rise to the governor's mansion and became perhaps the most powerful and influential governor in the state's history. The liberal faction of the state's Democratic Party would continue to challenge conservative hegemony, but they were never able to truly seize power. The conservatives had effectively won the "war after the war."

"Massive Resistance," Texas, and the NAACP

THE CAMPAIGN TO END INSTITUTIONAL, legal segregation, "Jim Crow" as it is often known, in Texas and the rest of the South was a long and bitter campaign. Southern state governments established segregationist laws that governed almost all aspects of public life and interaction as quickly as they could when Reconstruction ended. Such laws became dominant throughout the South from the early 1870s through the 1890s as an attempt at their own "brand" of reconstruction: the re-entrenchment of the concept of white superiority as a method of uniting all whites, while at the same time diminishing any class divisions that existed among whites. Such a social construction allowed white elite elements—land owners, business leaders, wealthy merchants, and politicians—to continue to dominate southern society even though they constituted only a small slice of the populace. Put another way, southern society divided along racial instead of class lines.

The legality of "Jim Crow" in the South rested upon a Supreme Court decision, the notorious *Plessy v. Ferguson* decision in 1896 that enshrined the legal concept of "separate but equal." For years civil rights groups brought a number of legal actions challenging the "separate but equal" clause, but with little success. The NAACP became the lead organization involved in these legal confrontations, and despite a lack of full success, the group continued to persist. Victory in such cases began to come when Thurgood Marshall became the lead litigator for the NAACP. Marshall changed the organization's legal strategy in the years immediately after World War II. Instead of contesting political oppression, Marshall decided that the weakest chink in the segregationist armor protecting "Jim Crow" was education. The denial of equality in education was a concept that resonated with a majority of Americans (at least those outside the South), and in Marshall's mind was an issue that would also find favor with at least the higher courts.

Marshall's new stratagem began to pay dividends as he won a number of narrow decisions that began to weaken school segregation. He was now ready to argue a case that would end the foundation of legal segregation. He did so in the 1954 landmark *Brown v. Board of Education, Topeka* case. Marshall's argument was brilliant. He attacked separate education as "inherently unequal," which meant that the quality or pervasiveness of the facilities and instruction was not an issue. Instead, the maintenance of a separate system deemed one of those—"black schools—innately inferior. The Supreme Court agreed with Marshall and struck down *Plessy* in a unanimous 9-0 decision. Southern schools, the Court later ruled, had to desegregate with "all deliberate speed."

Southern states were not going to give up Jim Crow that easily, and thus they pledged "Massive Resistance," to a Supreme Court decision that they called "an abuse of judicial power," and an attempt to "encroach upon the reserved rights of the states." Southern communities began to organize "White Citizen's Councils"—bodies Thurgood Marshall called the "uptown Klan"— that consisted of lawyers, bankers, physicians, and civic officials who began to devise tactics to subvert integration efforts. Citing the need to "maintain business," and in the interest of "economic progress," these White Citizen's Councils provided money and civic support to any attempts to end Jim Crow. They ran "cover" for the political leaders to oppose federal action.

Texas governor Allan Shivers was one of those officials. He "invented" the concept of "interposition" to oppose a federal court order to desegregate the public schools in Mansfield; he even went as far to threaten to close "every public school in the state" if he had to in order to maintain segregation, which he called "the natural order of humanity." Texas' governor had put the state squarely on the front lines in the fight against desegregation. Texas' attorney general, John Ben Shepperd would then use another gambit in the fight, this time against the NAACP.

The NAACP had led the fight against Jim Crow, and thus to John Ben Shepperd that was who he had to stop. Elected in 1952, Shepperd was an obdurate segregationist. He had delivered an *amicus curae* brief on behalf of the state opposing Marshall's argument in *Brown*, and after that decision he helped to organize a working group of southern attorneys generals to create a legal strategy to stop any implementation of desegregation of public schools. As the state's chief legal officer, he defended Texas' segregated school system in numerous court cases, but it was exhaustive work and, generally, federal courts sided against Texas. Thus, he decided on a new tactic.

He went to a friendly court in Tyler and first received a temporary injunction that barred the NAACP from being a party to any desegregation suit in Texas. Thurgood Marshall and his associates kept defeating Shepperd in court, so he decided to keep them from participating. He then began coordinated attacks against the state NAACP. He conducted a raid and seized the association's records, a tactic designed to intimidate, and he then filed a lawsuit against the NAACP to ban them from "doing business" in Texas. The official charge was failure to pay the franchise tax—which as a non-profit they were actually exempt—and "inciting lawsuits" under the principle of barratry. The NAACP, thus, had to defend their actions.

The suit was filed in Tyler, a courtroom that was unquestionably hostile to the NAACP. The trial was lengthy, cost a great deal of money, and smacked of intimidation. In the end, the court found against the NAACP, which greatly limited their effectiveness. Shepperd then wrote a series of bills that friendly legislators introduced and the legislature passed that essentially made the NAACP a dormant organization in the state. "Massive Resistance" in Texas became one of intimidation and using the law to subvert the Supreme Court and Constitutional principles. It would not be until the late 1960s that federal courts would be able to end Texas' egregious practices to keep African Americans from exercising their granted Constitutional rights.

A Game that Was Not Just a Game

WHEN ANY DISCUSSION OF CIVIL RIGHTS in this nation comes up, most of the discourse begins with events, people, or political developments such as the *Plessy v. Ferguson* Supreme Court decision, the instigation of Jim Crow segregation, Rosa Parks, Emmett Till, Martin Luther King, Jr., the "March on Washington," and a myriad of other transformative actions that helped to usher in a new era of race relations in the United States. All the aforementioned incidents and persons are absolutely worthy of note, but I think that we often forget how another cultural activity played a large role in racial progress in our country—that of sports.

When Jackie Robinson broke the "color barrier" in Major League Baseball it was a huge milestone because baseball was truly the "national pastime" in 1947 and the presence of a man of African descent in the Major Leagues provided an enormous social comment. In fact, it was no coincidence that Jackie Robinson became a major league baseball player in 1947 and President Harry Truman—via executive order—integrated the nation's armed forces. There are countless other incidents in which sports and racial relations intersected and helped advance the cause of equality: the quiet but powerful 1968 Olympic protest of a raised fist on the medal stand by John Carlos and Tommie Smith that brought poignancy to a year and summer of simmering racial tension in the US; USC's Sam Cunningham's four touchdown performance against Alabama in 1970 that hastened legendary Crimson Tide head coach to finally bring black players to the premier program in the Southeastern Conference; and the struggles of African American golfers such as Lee Elder, Pete Brown, and

Charlie Sifford to break the "Caucasian only clause" of the PGA Tour. Another of those social altering events was the triumph of Texas Western University (now the University of Texas-El Paso) over the University of Kentucky in the 1966 NCAA Basketball Championship.

Today a spectator or a viewer would not think twice about seeing African Americans in any sports arena, venue, or field, but through the 1960s—due to segregationist policies—it was still a rare occurrence and in the American South major college sports was still almost completely all-white. Such a reality is why that 1966 championship game was so significant. Coach Don Haskins' Texas Western Miners would become the first team in which all five starters were African American to win the NCAA championship. And in the process, they defeated an all-white squad from the University of Kentucky, a member of the Southeastern Conference which restricted blacks from playing collegiate sports, and coached by Adolph Rupp, known as "The Baron" and at the time the winningest college basketball coach in history.

Texas Western University had always been a bit of an oddity when it came to Texas institutions of higher learning in that it had begun admitting African Americans and other ethnic groups much earlier than other Texas state supported schools. When Don Haskins arrived to coach the Miners' basketball team in 1961 his team already had three black players—one of whom was Nolan Richardson, who would go on to a legendary coaching career at the University of Tulsa and the University of Arkansas—and the university had been admitting black students for close to a decade. Haskins immediately had good teams, and he quickly saw the benefit of recruiting and playing black athletes, particularly those who grew up playing basketball in northern cities, which had become incubators for cutting edge basketball talent. Haskins' 1962-63 team made the NCAA tournament, as did the 1963-64 squad. His 1964-65 team, made up almost entirely of underclassmen, just missed the tournament, but did play and do well in the, at the time, almost equally competitive National Invitational Tournament.

Those underclassmen in 1965 had become seasoned veterans, so Haskins looked forward to having a strong team in 1965-66. Haskins continually insisted that he was not trying to make a statement, he just "wanted to put [his] five best guys on the court," and it just so happened that his five best players were black—in fact his seven best players, the ones who played the most minutes—were African American. While it may not have made a difference to Haskins, it did to much of the rest of the nation. African American players took the court at other schools outside the South, but racial stereotypes and racist attitudes still followed any player who dribbled a ball and did not have white skin. Coaches, analysts, and pundits recognized the talent of black players, but most also insisted that those players needed the "steadying, sensible hand" of white teammates. One prominent college coach once remarked that he could "easily win fifteen games with one of those Negro players from up north, and with two of 'em I could probably win twenty-twenty-five games. But, hell, if I had to play more than that I would *lose* twenty games. They just don't have any discipline." Perry Wallace, who became the first black player in Adolph Rupp's Southeastern Conference in an interview long after his playing days said, "'Nigger ball' they used to call it. Whites thought that if you put five blacks on the court at the same time they would revert to their 'native impulses' and play a very undisciplined brand of ball."

When Texas Western took the court that night with Bobby Joe Hill, David Lattin, Orsten Artis, Willie Worsley, and Harry Flournoy as the starters many of the spectators in the Cole Field House at the University of Maryland could not believe what they were seeing. One sportswriter could not help himself and he said aloud, "He's really going to do it!" And they did it well. Despite the stereotypes, the Miners played in a very deliberate, well-structured style, one that relied more on defense and a strong physical inside game than on flash, speed, and the rest of the typecast variety of play that racist and insensitive elements often called "jungle style." Texas Western, behind the brilliant outside play of leading scorer Bobby Joe Hill, and the strong low post game of David Lattin, overwhelmed Rupp's Wildcats and they won convincingly. They proved that African American players belonged in college basketball, and they changed the way the game was played.

A World's Fair in Texas: HemisFair '68

I WAS REMINDED THAT TEXAS' FIRST and only World's Fair happened in San Antonio on a recent trip to the Alamo City. I overheard a young boy ask his father what that 'big round tower thing" was in the distance. I took it that the young family had probably just arrived at the hotel, and perhaps were not frequent visitors to the Alamo City as the young man's dad answered, "I don't know, son." Many of you are currently saying to yourself that the child had no doubt spied the Tower of the Americas, one of the most distinctive elements of San Antonio's skyline and a reminder that San Antonio once hosted a World's Fair, the HemisFair '68 celebration that, to a large extent, introduced San Antonio to the world.

HemisFair was a commemoration of the 250th anniversary of the founding of San Antonio, and was the result of a long campaign to bring a World's Fair to Texas. The idea began in 1959 with some of the leading members of San Antonio's business and political community. San Antonio Congressman Henry B. Gonzalez helped to secure financing from federal agencies and the United States Congress, and the Texas State Legislature also chipped in some funds. The remainder of the costs came from private fund raising efforts, most from a consortium of twenty-six local banks. Ultimately, San Antonio's businessmen and citizens pledged more than five million dollars to HemisFair, a very significant sum in the early 1960s. A special fair non-profit company began in 1962, with William R. Sinkin as president.

Site selection proved to be one of the most difficult tasks. Organizers wanted to hold the exposition near the historic center of San Antonio, but the neighborhood surrounding downtown had badly deteriorated. Eventually they chose a ninety-acre site on the southeastern edge of downtown, and then applied for federal urban renewal funds to clear and reconstruct the area. The national government responded with large amounts of federal dollars to purchase houses and dilapidated businesses in the region. They were then razed and pavilions and fair buildings constructed in their place.

The city also had to prepare for the millions of visitors who would stream into San Antonio to attend the fair. The city and the state quickly upgraded its infrastructure, improving and building new roads and freeway ramps. Corporations and private individuals led a hotel construction boom in the downtown area. One amazing feat was the rapid construction of what would become the Hilton Palacio Del Rio Hotel, a luxury hostelry on the famed Riverwalk. In order to be ready for occupancy when the fair opened the contractor, the H.B. Zachry Company, designed and completed the structure in an amazing two hundred working days. Most of the rooms were fully built off-site as modules and lifted into place with a crane. The workers completed the placement of those modular rooms in an unprecedented forty-six days.

HemisFair opened on April 6, 1968 with the "Confluence of Civilizations in the Americas" as its theme. The Fair capitalized on San Antonio's great ethnic diversity, but it also highlighted San Antonio, and Texas, as a center of future international commerce and special cooperation between the United States and Latin America. More than thirty nations built and occupied pavilions, including Mexico, Canada, Japan, Italy, and Spain. The United States had a grand pavilion, built with $7.5 million from congressional legislation. The largest pavilion was the one sponsored by the state of Texas, a building that today is occupied by the outstanding Institute of Texan Cultures.

The centerpiece of HemisFair was the Tower of the Americas, the structure that so impressed that young boy in 2012. Its construction was also revolutionary. Its most distinctive feature, the round "tophouse" that today contains a restaurant and an observation deck, was built on the ground and then moved to the top with twenty-four steel lifting rods.

During its run, HemisFair hosted exhibits and presentations that highlighted space exploration, Latin American folk art, a production of Verdi's *Don Carlo*, art from the Prado in Madrid, and appearances by the Ballet Folklorico de Mexico and the Bolshoi Ballet. Corporations such as Kodak, Coca-Cola, and Gulf Oil presented a number of events and exhibitions, all which emphasized the partnerships that fostered friendship between the countries of the Americas.

HemisFair's financial underwriting was impressive, over $150 million, but the exposition (like most of its kind) lost money. Officials had greatly overestimated attendance, although it did attract more than 6 million visitors. It also brought San Antonio a great deal of notoriety, which played a large role in that city's business boom of the 1970s and 1980s. The permanent buildings of the site became the most enduring contribution of HemisFair, and today it forms a vital part of San Antonio's downtown tourist industry.

HemisFair also "re-introduced" San Antonio and Texas to the world. The Kennedy assassination, the legacy of Jim Crow, and an image that often emphasized a pre-industrial past instead of a progressive future had hindered Texas as a site for futuristic and modern processes and corporations. Events such as HemisFair began to change such perceptions; San Antonio today is a headquarters city of a number of Fortune 500 companies. So, in a way, when that young man asked his father what that "tower thing" was, he could have answered that it pointed a way to the city's future.

Greed and Scandal in the Legislature: The Sharpstown Incident

ONE-PARTY DEMOCRATIC DOMINANCE WAS THE norm in Texas politics for over a century after Reconstruction, and it was not until the 1990s that the Republican Party truly became competitive within the state. Today one could argue that Texas is back to one-party rule, but the ones in charge are on the other side of the aisle. There are many reasons why the shift began, ones that are complex and varied, but one of the first "chinks in the armor" of Democratic control came with the Sharpstown scandal of 1971-72.

Like so many political scandals, Sharpstown began inauspiciously. In January of 1971, the Securities and Exchange Commission (SEC) filed a suit that charged stock fraud against attorney general Waggoner Carr, former state insurance commissioner John Osario, and Frank Sharp, a Houston businessman who owned, among other things, the Sharpstown State Bank and National Bankers Life. When the suit was initially brought it generated little attention outside of Austin, and many people thought it was just one more instance of an overzealous federal government. Such would not be the case.

When the SEC's lawyers began to reveal their case, shock waves hit Texas politics. The federal case included some serious accusations against not only the figures named in the action, but also implicated prominent state officials such as Elmer Baum, a member of the state bank board, and Forth Worth legislator Tommy Shannon. But the most astounding dignitaries linked to the charges were Speaker of the House Gus Mutscher, Jr. and Governor Preston Smith.

The SEC alleged that Frank Sharp had concocted an elaborate scheme that would allow him and various state officials to grab lucrative profits from state action. Sharp granted over $600,000 in loans to the accused officials, and in turn those officials used the funds to buy stock in National Bankers Life (NBL). Sharp, in his capacity as the head of NBL, wildly overinflated the value of the company's stock, which could then be resold at a huge profit. Furthermore, the plan depended on some favorable banking bills passing the legislature, and that happened when Smith placed them on the agenda of a 1969 special session, and Mutscher and Shannon forced the legislation through the legislature with little discussion or debate. Smith actually vetoed the bills, but not until after he and Baum took extravagant profits. It was not just bribery but rather an intricate case of fraud and subversion of law that took advantage of the minutiae and Byzantine nature of state government that was only be possible because there was virtually no opposition to those who controlled the levers of power.

The case and scandal grew even more intense when it came to light that Sharp and Lieutenant Governor Ben Barnes, the young, influential, rising star of Democratic state politics, enjoyed a close relationship. Barnes, as lt. governor, controlled the agenda of the state senate and with both Mutscher and Smith also involved, Frank Sharp had the entire apparatus of state government under his thumb. Political pressure to distance themselves and explain their actions increased exponentially on all involved, but particularly on Barnes and Smith, two men who disliked each other and were expected to face-off in the upcoming governor's race.

State law enforcement officials moved quickly to make their own case in the scandal. Carr, Baum, and Sharp's fate was left to the federal officials, but since the actions in the legislature did not specifically violate federal securities law, the state chose to indict Mutscher, Shannon, and Rush McGinty, a Mutscher aide, on bribery charges. Smith and Barnes escaped state and federal charges, although most Texans considered them just as guilty and culpable in the scandal, if not more so. Travis County District Attorney R.O. Smith (the official in charge of the prosecution) named Smith as an unindicted co-conspirator.

A state judge moved the trial from Austin to Abilene, and it got underway in February 1972. The case was mostly circumstantial, and it involved a number of intricate legal maneuvers and jargon that was almost indecipherable to the public. Eventually, the jury found Mutscher and his co-defendants guilty on all counts. The presiding judge sentenced all three to five years probation, which effectively ended Gus Mutscher's political career.

The former speaker was not the only political casualty. Preston Smith and Ben Barnes did both run for governor in the 1972 election, but the taint of scandal doomed both their candidacies and neither man made the election run-off. In the end, political newcomer Dolph Briscoe—part of the conservative faction of the party—won the nomination in an unexpected and very tight run-off against the liberal reform candidate Frances "Sissy" Farenthold. William P. Hobby, Jr., a moderate reformer, took over as the lieutenant governor, and scores of young, reform minded politicians filled the state legislature. New attorney general John Hill became perhaps the most liberal person to ever fill that important office. As author Charles Deaton termed it, Texas voters "threw the rascals out," and it looked as if a new, more liberal Texas electoral landscape might be on the horizon.

Pundits who predicted such an outcome misread Texas' voters. Certainly, the scandal incensed the public's ire against the "old guard," which superficially indicated a readiness of Texas' voters to turn toward the reform faction of the party. What many forgot was that Texans are, by and large, a conservative people, and the many voters who turned away from the establishment Democrats because of Sharpstown moved not to the reform faction but toward the growing state Republican Party. Briscoe would serve two terms in office, but in 1978 Texas, a state that had not elected a Republican governor since 1870, gave Republican William Clements a surprise victory over attorney general John Hill, which signaled the beginning of a competitive two-party system in Texas. Sharpstown was not the only reason for the change, but it was one of the most important.

IV: Reflection

The Five Most Transformative Events in Texas History: One Man's List

SOMEONE ONCE TOLD ME, AND I THINK it was the late Don Walker, but it could have also been Mike Campbell, that for the most part historians are at least benign, and on occasion can be genteel. That said, the surest and fastest way to start a fight—and sometimes a literal fight, not a figurative or rhetorical one—is to stand up in a group of Texas historians and say one of two things: "Is Texas a western or southern state," or "How exactly did Crockett die." After an experience I had at a West Texas Historical Association meeting once in Alpine many years ago I might add giving a paper or a talk that in any way suggests that most of what we believe about the "cowboy" is a myth. The point I am taking a roundabout way to making is that for Texans many things are almost sacrosanct, something that you do not question or do not touch, and when we have disagreements over something it is almost never a small argument but almost a full blown, yelling, brouhaha.

Well, the last thing I want to do is start a fight. So, I will not regale you with those earlier sobering questions. Instead, in the spirit of the current political environment of the nation let me wade into waters that are wholly subjective, and quite often solely personal—but I'll do so with the conviction of a zealot and the confidence of a television evangelist. What I bring today is what one Texas historian—me—thinks are the five most transformative events in Texas history.

First, a caveat. I have intentionally used the word "transformative," and not significant. In many cases, and I think this is so, the items I have included I may place in both lists. But then again, if you pressed me I might include something like Mexican Independence and the subsequent decision to give Stephen F. Austin an empresario grant as one of the most significant events, but perhaps not necessarily "transformative," for nothing more than the fact that I believe that American intrusion would have eventually occurred, and the eventual result of revolution against Mexico would have also most likely occurred. Thus, it is significant, but not necessarily transformative. Webster's New World dictionary defines "transformative" thusly: "to undergo a change in form, appearance, or character." Such a definition was the starting line for my list. We all know that there are very few times in the past in which we can draw a line and categorically state that everything after that event was different. Such a demarcation would be the ultimate in transformation. More likely, in historical terms, we can better declare that such events altered conditions enough that it changed the development and direction of a historical path. That is more the aim of this talk.

My purpose here is to bring to you something that would not only intrigue you, but also come up with your own questions and ideas about the topic. That is, of course, what makes history fun and keeps us coming to such events and keeps us involved. I also wanted to use my "list" to advance some of the current "cutting edge" thought in the most recent trends of Texas' historical literature. Some historians call it "shifting the narrative," or using revision as a way to "update" our understanding of the past. Historian Ty Cashion, in his masterful work *Lone Star Mind* goes further and calls for the development of a new "meta-narrative," one that is not as reliant on the more traditional interpretation of Teas history being a part of the pervasive movement of American ideas and culture across the continent, one that relies on a foundation of Anglo-Saxon, Christian, male dominance to form a unique people and history. Rightly, Cashion and others note that such a past is not "usable" in the twenty-first century, and it is increasingly one that has no relevance to a state that is fast becoming one of the most multi-cultural and multi-ethnic enclaves in the nation. According to the U.S. Census it is not New York, San Francisco, or even Los Angeles that is the most ethnically diverse city in the United States, but it is Houston, Texas—a fact that when you inform those not from Texas (or probably many in the Texas legislature or our state's representatives in Congress) shocks the hell out of them.

Certainly, my list is somewhat personal, what I think have been those points in our past that have been important in shaping Texas into the place it is today. As you will see, four of my five events took place in the 20th century, and if we are trying to present a "usable" past then I think that is appropriate. It was during the 20th century that Texas matured, and it was during that era that what makes Texas important in the U.S. and the world, which is how our modern economy grew, but more importantly the society and culture that economy spawned, has been most responsible for producing the Texas we recognize today. Put another way, while we may revere the Alamo as some sort of icon, the battle in that former mission does not have much effect on the way we live our lives today. But, the gusher discovered at Spindletop in 1901, and the industry it ushered in, certainly does.

So, we are about ready to begin our list, but as anyone who has perhaps listened to one of those old radio countdown shows, or watches that genre of television shows that showcase a certain year or decade (I am particularly fond of the those old VH1 programs about the 80s, a decade in which I was a hundred pounds lighter and had even more and "taller" hair), you know that quite often they begin with some items that "almost made the list," so I think I may do the same. I would be willing to bet that some of those are ones you would have put on your register. Some of you may find some of these entries a bit strange, so I will also offer a little explanation why I think they may be transformative. And again, I offer the following: this is my list, my ideas. So, wait and don't close the book just yet.

Certainly, a list of "significance" would include something about Spaniards and European contact. The collision of the Spanish and Native American peoples began a centuries long clash of civilizations and cultures, one that would eventually lead to virtual extermination for one group, and an almost three century sovereignty for the other. It was transformative, but because I have limited the list to five, I have to make choices and I chose to not include this one. However, it would not take much to convince me to include it.

Another close one is the Civil War and Reconstruction, for obvious reasons. The Civil War and its aftermath certainly transformed Texas, and the South along with it. If this little exercise concerned only the South then it would be on here without a doubt. You could make the argument that it still should. After all, the War ended slavery and the planter hegemony, and Reconstruction shaped much of how Texans viewed the function of government and its relationship with the national entity. And if we were speaking about Texas two or three decades ago I might have placed it in the Top Five. But, while it was transformative, in my mind it just misses.

Another one, and this is representative of the power of one single event, is the Kennedy assassination. When JFK was shot and killed on Commerce Street in Dallas, Texas began slang for hatred, a place that killed the young champion of Camelot with its extreme right leaning radicalism and its "cowboy culture." It didn't matter that much of that reputation came from stereotype and exaggeration (much of it drive by Texans), the world believed it and the state had to deal with it. Texas, by necessity had to do some introspection that day, and it had to come up with some answers. So, close, but not quite.

Related to the previous event is one more esoteric, and that is the Dallas Cowboys becoming "America's Team." For better or worse, the NFL is the nation's sport, when the Cowboys became the darling the of the nation it went a long toward overcoming the stigma of the JFK assassination. It mattered, too, that the Cowboys were seen as innovative and modern. If they were, then Texas was as well.

This one may take a little imagination, but how about the founding of Southwest Airlines? It reduced the size of Texas first, but then became the leader of a new transportation revolution. Southwest became the face of the new airline industry in the U.S., and all this from a little Texas company that refused to give up.

Now, without further adieu, my list. They are in chronological order, not importance. So, here we go:

1. **1836: The Battle of San Jacinto**: I suppose that this number could be the entire Texas Revolution, but I chose this one battle for a reason. While the Texians had, for the most part, been successful against meager Mexican troops in 1835, 1836 and the arrival of Santa

Anna had been a different story. After decimating the small garrison at the Alamo, Santa Anna and Mexican forces had terrorized the country side during the "Runway Scrape" through March 1836. At the same time, another Mexican force under General Urrea had roundly defeated and then executed James W. Fannin's forces in South Texas. Sam Houston's main army ran the real risk of being caught between the two armies, which would have no doubt led to a crushing defeat and a quick end of the Texas Revolution.

But in early April, Houston and the Texas Army caught a break, largely through Santa Anna's hubris. Confident that Houston's rag-tag force was not a real threat, Santa Anna split his force and sent one group under General Vincente Filisola toward the settlements in East Texas (specifically Nacogdoches) and in the direction of Houston's march, while he would chase after the interim Texas government near Galveston Bay and eventually link with Urrea's troops.

Houston was waiting on just such an opportunity. He reversed course, caught Santa Anna on the plain between the San Jacinto River and Buffalo Bayou, and in just 18 minutes on April 21, 1836 roundly defeated Santa Anna, captured the Mexican president, and secured for Texas independence. Without a doubt, if that had not occurred the course of Texas and U.S. history would have been drastically altered. Texas would be a part of the U.S., but it would have probably been a gain of the Mexican War, which would also have meant that Texas, which had the presence of slaves, would have become a big part of the debate over slavery in those western territories. That very well could have led to the Civil War ten or fifteen years before it did begin, and that would have meant a very different outcome.

2. **Spindletop**: No industry, no commercial activity, not cotton, not cattle, not the railroads have meant more to Texas than petroleum. The story of twentieth century Texas is, in many ways, a story of oil. Before the discovery of and the large-scale extraction of petroleum Texas was largely a poor, backwater, state that generally followed in the pattern of the southern states. It was rural, agrarian, and lacked standard basic services such as even a rudimentary educational

system, decent roads and infrastructure, and cities with a viable economy outside one spent trading agricultural commodities. Oil allowed Texas to escape that pattern and become more urban, allocate much more revenue to state services, and—probably most importantly—it established a foundation for industrialization in the middle of the 20th century that other southern states did not have. I maintain that oil extraction is a leading factor that made Texas—at least economically and somewhat socially if not culturally and politically—a western instead of a southern state.

So, perhaps Spindletop as an event is more symbolic than significant, but when Anthony Lucas' gusher blew in on January 10, 1901 it marked the arrival of a new era in Texas. Beaumont and Port Arthur immediately became boom towns of a proportion Texas had never seen. The industry moved out from its footprint in the Golden Triangle to the area north and east of Houston. Ross Sterling, for example, founded a drilling company that he named for the small town, Humble, near his first field. That company would go on to become a major player in the American petroleum industry and, through a merger with John Rockefeller's Standard Oil, would form a new corporate giant that today is known as Exxon, the largest corporation in the world, and one that in 1985—after years away—moved its headquarters back to its roots in Texas. Another group of investors in the region formed a new company that they named for the state—the Texas Company, today known as Texaco.

Texas became the leading state in oil production, passing Oklahoma, California, and Louisiana, in the early 1920s (a title it has never relinquished) when wildcat drillers discovered vast fields in north Texas, the Panhandle, and then the monumental Permian Basin deposits in West Texas. The vast and prolific East Texas Oil field came on line with Dad Joiner and the Daisy Bradford #3, and after Letourneau industries developed a viable platform, Texas firms began to exploit finds in the Gulf of Mexico. Recently, hydraulic "fracking" and other methods of extracting petroleum from shale has caused a new renaissance in the industry, and Texas is in the forefront. Oil and Texas are synonymous.

But perhaps more consequential than anything else, those oil dollars produced in Texas were largely deposited in Texas banks, they bought policies and funded Texas insurance companies, and oil workers and newly wealthy land owners spent money in Texas department and clothing stores and they built homes in Texas cities. Ask the people at Neiman-Marcus (if they have anyone left there with any institutional memory) about how important oil money was to their fortunes. Most importantly, those banks, insurance companies and other entities loaned money to Texas businesses, creating a symbiotic relationship that helped move Texas from a poor state with not much real national economic importance, to one of the most dynamic economies in the nation. It was oil, and the foundation it built, that allowed Texas to cease being a colony of eastern and world capital and take a seat on the world economic stage. So, perhaps I am making Spindletop a symbol for the whole industry, but it was in that little wetland between Beaumont and Port Arthur that Texas began the trek to modernity that still resonates today. I am not sure it is not the *most* important single event in the state's history.

3. **World War II**: No one could possibly argue that World War II was not transformative for the world, the United States, or Texas. When the United States entered the war against Germany and Japan on December 8, 1941, it began an era that would alter almost everything we knew and thought about the world we lived in. When it was over almost fifty million people were dead, the map of the world was changed, the nuclear age was upon us, and it almost immediately spawned a decades long Cold War between the U.S. and the Soviets that would be as significant and transformative as the war that generated it.

Most notable, over 750,000 Texans went to war by the end in 1945. Over 22,000 of them did not come back. The men who served in the Thirty-Sixth Infantry Division, the Ninetieth Division, and the First, Second, and Third Armored Divisions, as well as in the Air Corps, the Marines, Navy, Coast Guard, and Merchant Marines, along with the women of the WACS and WAVES never forgot their service, what they saw, or how their lives were forever changed. It is always amazing to me when I think about those young men—and the majority were so young—having to go off to fight such a widespread and consequential war. Did they know the depth of the importance of what they were doing?

A number of Texans became household names during the war. Chester Nimitz became the commander of the Pacific Fleet and directed the successful campaign to defeat the Japanese. William Simpson commanded the Ninth Army during the march across France and Germany and was instrumental in fortifying the lines and attacking the Nazis in the Ardennes at the Battle of the Bulge. Claire Chennault left teaching high school behind to form the famous Flying Tigers that fought with the Chinese against Japan in in the early days of the war. Doris Miller, relegated to being a mess mate in the Navy simply because of his race, manned deck guns at Pearl Harbor and became one of the first heroes of the war before he died in the Pacific. Oveta Culp Hobby developed the Women's Army Corps and became the highest ranking woman during the war. And of course Audie Murphy, all 5'5" of him, became the most decorated soldier of the war, and his acts of bravery still resonate today.

As notable as the people of World War II were, the war transformed Texas at home even more. Along the Gulf Coast rose great shipbuilding and petrochemical plants, as well as refineries to provide the fuel for war. Texas built upon its petroleum foundation and became even more the center of the industry. Yes, Alabama had ship yards, and Mississippi and Louisiana training bases and some war-time industry, Texas became the southern state that benefitted the most from the war. It expanded the industrial base of the state that began with the modern oil industry. The war also revitalized the paper and wood-pulp industry in East Texas, it brought the world's largest tin smelter in Texas City, and Texas farmers began to prosper as they never had before as prices skyrocketed and mechanization helped to increase production.

Texas had been important to the nascent aircraft industry at the turn of the century, but World War II solidified that relationship.

Texas weather and physical geography had made it a natural place to train pilots, and the federal government continued to utilize Texas as a training base for airmen just as it had during World War I. San Antonio became the center of American air power training, but at least fifteen other Texas cities saw either training or bombing ranges located in their vicinity. Those federal dollars helped to boost and expand Texas' economy to heights it had never before reached. And to increase access to those federal contracts, aircraft manufactures built plants in Texas. Garland, Grand Prairie and Fort Worth became the locations for such facilities. The Consolidated Vultee (later Convair) plant in Fort Worth had an assembly line that was a mile long, and from that line rolled thousands of B-24s, one of the most versatile aircrafts in American history.

The federal government actually contributed more than many Texans want to admit. Texas was the location of POW camps, training camps, and the aforementioned aircraft facilities. Texas' powerful congressmen did their just duty in bringing federal largesse to the Lone Star State. Those petrochemical, rubber, tin, and paper plants? Their largest receipts came in the form of federal contracts. Thus, federal money paid salaries and left money in Texas, dollars that would help to make the state one of the most dynamic economies in the nation.

Perhaps the most important development of the war years was the acceleration of the growing rural-urban shift in the state. The shift had begun during the Depression, and the war made the movement even more dramatic. People moved to Texas in record numbers to take those jobs in the factories, almost half a million in the four years of the war. But more than that, rural Texans left the farms and ranches and came to Texas' cities in droves. While Texas' overall population grew by 20.2% between 1940 and 1950, the shift in cities was more dramatic. Corpus Christi for example had a population of 27,000 in 1930, and by 1950 had just under 110,000 people. Houston, already Texas' largest city with just under 300,000 in 1930 doubled to 600,000 by 1950. Lubbock had 20,000 in 1930, and by 1950 was on the cusp of 75,000. Those examples were typical all over the state.

The larger point is that WWII forever made Texas a modern state, one that could take its place among the economic and social giants of the nation. It was a transformation that was almost unnerving because it happened so quickly. The state rushed to get its infrastructure up to date, and it also had to move—not wholly, but some—away from the politics of the Old South and more toward a modern version. That did not mean that Texas would acquiesce in modifying its bi-racial policies of segregation and oppression, but it did mean that the state and its people would certainly have to confront them in ways that they never had before. All in all, the epitome of a transformative event.

4. **Jack S. Kilby invents the integrated circuit**: Another great benefit of the oil industry was that it brought a great number of educated professionals to Texas. Oil companies hired geologists, engineers, accountants, managers, pilots, and more to help them extract petroleum from the earth. While Texas had always been a place of great in-migration, most of those who came were not much different from those who already lived here—mostly southern, mostly rural, and mostly poor. This migration was much different since it was not southern (in fact it was mostly Midwestern and northern), was more urban, and more educated and middle class. It was also an entrepreneurial class, one that believed in innovation and new business opportunities. These migrants would change drastically change Texas.

Two of those entrepreneurially inclined individuals, John Clarence Karcher and Eugene B. McDermott, would found a company that first developed and sold seismographic processes for the oil industry, but by 1951 would have a new name—Texas Instruments—and that company would in its employee have a man who would change not only the fate of Texas but of the world: Jack St. Clair Kilby.

I hope that you have heard of Kilby, but if not I know you have heard of his invention: the integrated circuit. Kilby, who came up with the idea of the circuit almost simultaneously and independently of another engineer in California by the name of Robert Noyce (and

I'll bet you have heard of his company, Intel), was a Missourian by birth and grew up in Kansas. In 1958 Kilby was a new employee at Texas Instruments, and as such he did not have the right to a summer vacation. So, he spent his time working on the problem that everyone in his field was trying to solve—how to manufacture electrical circuits in such a manner that they could be cheap to produce as well as efficient. The solution that he worked out that summer was to place the circuits on a single piece of semiconductor material. He used germanium, while Noyce in California used silicon, but the principle behind both were the same. Texas Instruments became the leading producer of integrated circuits (they placed most of theirs in hand-held calculators). Kilby's invention would eventually become the cornerstone of the new computer and electronic industry, which would fundamentally change the American economy. Texas, thus, would become one of the leading states of this new technology, and before the recent boom high tech companies contributed more to the state treasury than did oil.

5. **Michael Dell/Dell Computers**: Kilby's and Texas Instrument's innovations made Texas an important place for high tech, but one man and one company would that utilized Kilby's innovation would make Texas almost the center of the industry. Michael Dell grew up in Houston and would eventually enroll at the University of Texas. Dell was typical of the "first wave" of computer entrepreneurs; he got his first calculator (a TI model) when he was 7, and convinced his parents to buy him am Apple II when he was 15. When he brought it home he immediately disassembled it to see how it worked. While at the University of Texas he began to sell upgrade kits for personal computers out of his dorm room. Eventually, he gained a contract to provide computers to the State of Texas, which helped to launch his company Dell Computers in North Austin. At first he sold his computers only by phone of mail order, assembling each one as orders were placed. By 1996, he was selling his units over the internet, and in 2001 he had grown so much that Dell became the largest personal computer company in the world.

Michael Dell is on this list because to a large degree he represents the "New Texan." Entrepreneurial and an innovator, Dell's Texas is the reason why the state's economy is so strong, precisely because it tends to eschew old models and traditional ways of doing business. It embraces technology and the "can-do" attitude of the sole proprietorship, which makes it more responsive and more nimble to market trends. Texas' economy is strong because it is a forward looking region; its eyes are on the future, not on the past—and yes I know that is a strange thing for a historian to say. The new Texas is one that will have to deal with new trends, new political realities, and new arrangements. It is really no longer the arena of the wildcat Texas oilman, J.R. Ewing, if you will, but instead of a global capitalist negotiated a new form of neo-liberalism. And instead of a cowboy hat, he very well may have a pony tail and wear sandals.

So there you have it, my list. As I said at the beginning, it is highly personal, but I think it is representative of what makes Texas, Texas—past, present, and future.

A Struggle Just to Survive:
African American Colleges in Texas

THE CONCEPT OF WHITE SUPERIORITY, as practiced first in the Antebellum Old South and later during Reconstruction, Redemption, and the Jim Crow eras, had no greater ally than ignorance. The white, southern, elite hegemony fully understood that a person who lacks education was a person who could be dominated and subjugated—thus their conscious attempts to deny a full education to African Americans after the end of slavery. Southern leaders certainly attempted to keep people of African descent away from any form of higher education, but African Texans worked just as diligently to gain access to institutions of higher learning. As you can imagine, white Texans of the late nineteenth and early twentieth century refused to open their schools to blacks, so African Americans created their own institutions, which began a rich heritage of historically black universities in Texas.

Immediately following the Civil War, the federally established Freedmen's Bureau took the lead in instituting primary and high schools for freed slaves, and they were aided greatly by northern churches and black denominations such as the Colored Methodist Episcopal Church. The advancements were welcome, but it became obvious through the 1860s that any true progress would necessitate the establishment of institutions of higher learning.

The first such college established specifically for African Texans was Paul Quinn College, established in Austin in 1872 and named for a former Methodist bishop. Under the leadership of the African Methodist Episcopal Church, Paul Quinn's primary mission was to train pastors for black Methodist churches, although it also educated teachers and provided a full liberal arts program. The struggling school moved to Waco in 1877, where its principal function became instruction in vocational professions. It moved to Dallas in 1990, and today occupies the former campus of Bishop College.

Through the 1870s and 1880s a number of private black colleges began in Texas including Wiley College in Marshall (1873), Tillotson College in Austin (1881), Bishop College in Marshall (1881—moved to Dallas in 1961), Mary Allen College in Crockett (1886), Texas College in Tyler (1894), St. Phillips in San Antonio (1898), Butler College, also in Tyler (1905), and Jarvis College in Hawkins (1912). All of these institutions were church-affiliated schools and offered the same basic curriculum, primarily designed to train teachers for black schools, although—reflecting the prevailing idea of the time—most offered a limited vocational program.

The state of Texas actually built one of the earliest state-supported schools for blacks in the South with the opening of Prairie View State Normal School, which is now Prairie View A&M University, in 1878. A land-grant college located near Hempstead, Prairie View's instruction was primarily limited to agricultural and vocational training—exactly the role the white elite hegemony sought to limit blacks within—although it added teacher training in the 1880s. Constitutionally, and following the concept of "separate but equal," the state had promised to build and fund a fully functional liberal arts college on par with the University of Texas, but never had such an intention and kept Prairie View underfunded and out of view. However, the school did miraculously survive and still offers a quality higher education and a wide array of degrees and programs.

Texas Southern, the second state-supported historically black university, opened its doors as an attempt to maintain the concept of segregation. A lawsuit brought by Heman Sweatt in an attempt to desegregate the University of Texas' law school threatened to shatter the state's reliance on "separate but equal." The state legislature, in an attempt to influence the suit, allowed the state to take over Houston College for Negroes in 1947 and renamed it Texas State University for Negroes. They hastily authorized a law and graduate school, all in an attempt to keep the Supreme Court from ruling in Sweatt's favor. Their actions ultimately had no effect as the justices ordered UT to admit Sweatt. The new university remained, and in 1951 the name became Texas Southern University.

All of these institutions shared one thing in common: they struggled to find a financial foothold. While white colleges and universities of the day could depend on generous donations from wealthy benefactors, their African American counterparts had no such financial windfall. Whites either did not care if they survived, or explicitly hoped they would fail; the move from slavery to freedom did not create a significant black wealthy class that could underwrite such schools. Harassed, underfunded, and constantly struggling against great odds, perhaps the most phenomenal thing about these schools is that they did survive and they established a rich tradition of leadership. Education can serve as a great equalizer, and when a mass of Americans finally began to demand the South change its segregation ways many of the leaders instrumental in that struggle were granted their degrees and knowledge from these small but powerful institutions.

A Texas Gift to the Nation: The Origins of Juneteenth

"WHAT, TO THE AMERICAN SLAVE, is your Fourth of July?" I answer, a day that reveals to him, more than all other days in the year, the gross injustice and cruelty to which he is the constant victim." The above quote is from famed abolitionist Frederick Douglass in a speech he gave to an anti-slavery audience in 1852. Many readers today may superficially find such a sentiment harsh—perhaps unpatriotic—but if they will stop and think about the situation in America in 1852 they should understand that Douglass is referring to the hypocrisy of a day devoted to celebrating freedom while more than four million slaves in the United States did not have such liberty and were locked in a state of perpetual bondage. That is the context of the remark.

For those of African descent, there is another independence day, a day to celebrate the end of the brutal enslavement of human beings simply because they were of another race. That would be June 19th, better known as Juneteenth, and it is a holiday with its roots firmly in Texas soil.

With the end of the Civil War came the end of slavery. In most of the American South, Union troops occupied at least some territory and were able to force the end of slavery. But Texas was never truly occupied by invading Union troops, other than a brief period on Galveston Island, so the end of the war left no controlling force to enforce the new American law abolishing slavery. Thus, on June 19th, 1865, United States General Gordon Granger landed on Galveston Island and read aloud the Emancipation Proclamation, which immediately ended the enslavement of 250,000 African Texans. The news spread out from Galveston to the plantations of East and Central Texas and to the cities and towns across the state. The now former slaves, with their life-long prayers and pleadings of freedom now answered, broke out in spontaneous celebrations.

The significance and formal enshrining of the holiday arrived during the era of Reconstruction when African Texans and Freedman's Bureau officials used the occasion of Juneteenth to educate former slaves about voting rights and their newly won civil liberties. The rallies and forums soon came to be marked by picnics, speeches, dances, and dramatic interpretations. A new holiday celebrated by Texas' black citizens was born.

As the celebration evolved it came to symbolize an independence holiday. The hymn "Lift Every Voice" (the African American national anthem) became a standard at gatherings along with entertainment, pageants, parades, barbeques, and athletic contests. Music was *de rigueur* and a crucial part of the family atmosphere. Given the tenor of the times, celebrations were often relegated to the outskirts of cities and towns by the white hierarchy, who often viewed the celebration as an affront to their ideas of white superiority. African American communities began to raise funds to buy tracts of land to hold their celebrations, which quite often acquired the moniker of Emancipation Park. Through the years, Juneteenth became one of the most important days of the year within the African American community.

Time can take a toll, and by the 1960s Juneteenth began to decline in popularity. The push for integration sapped some of the interest, but perhaps the movement of mass numbers of African Texans out of small towns and the rural countryside contributed the most to the fall; urban settings are not the best venues for a holiday of picnics and outdoor ball games, and young people are often not as attuned to tradition when there is so much excitement swirling around them.

But a funny thing happened on the way to the end of Juneteenth—it experienced a revival. The rise of "black pride" movements and a desire to reconnect to one's origins in the 1970s and early 1980s led to a renewal of the Juneteenth holiday. The Texas legislature passed a bill in 1979 making Juneteenth an official state holiday and the state annually holds a state-sponsored celebration. Most importantly, Juneteenth spread outside the state's borders. As African Texans moved elsewhere they brought their independence holiday with them and introduced it in other locales. It is fast becoming an unofficial commemoration in places such as Oklahoma, Missouri, and California.

I wish Frederick Douglass could come back and attend a Juneteenth celebration. I would hope that he would see a country trying mightily to correct a past in which it is rightly not proud. We are moving toward a nation that understands and honors our multi-cultural heritage and way of life. To experience the joy of another form of independence, attend your local Juneteenth celebration. I know that I will. After all, it is a celebration of America—and the food is always pretty good as well!

A Texas Independence Day Tradition

INDEPENDENCE DAY, JULY 4TH, IS THE MOST significant of our national holidays. As the day we celebrate the founding of the United States, it is a day of fireworks, patriotic displays, parades, picnics, and family gatherings—everything that is good about a holiday. Naturally, in Texas we have another July 4th tradition, one that also involves festivities, but also has a large dose of something almost every Texan enjoys—music, lots of good music. Of course I am speaking of one of Texas' favorite sons, Willie Nelson, and his annual July 4th picnic.

During the late 1960s and the early 1970s, Willie Nelson was a relatively unknown country crooner, and if the mention of his name brought any recognition it was probably due to others, such as Patsy Cline, Ray Price, and Faron Young, recording songs he had written. The problem was that the Nashville "establishment" just didn't understand the eclectic artist from Abbott, Texas. He had different ideas about how country music should be written, staged, and sung—a vision that hardly any of the record executives shared with Nelson. In Willie's mind, the "Nashville Sound" that was at the time the rage among the music bosses and the predominant format on country radio was missing a huge audience—young people, honky-tonkers, hippies, and a multitude of others who just couldn't identify with a sound that was too slick, too produced, and had little if any "edge." The Nashville Sound may have played well in suburbia, but it was not a hit in the urban core, on campuses, and somewhat surprisingly, in the birthplace of country music, the rural countryside.

So, Willie and some of his fellow thinkers left Nashville and came back to Texas, where they began to initiate a new sound, "Outlaw" or Progressive Country. At first other than a few "hippie" fans in Austin, and at smaller venues around the state, music lovers ignored the "Outlaws." The new sub-genre took some time to gain acceptance, but an event that turned out much differently than its promoters had envisioned helped promote the new sound, and it also helped to spawn a Texas summer tradition.

The Woodstock music festival was still a fresh event in 1972, and promoters and visionaries in all genres of music had tried, with little success, to imitate the upstate New York phenomenon. Four promoters from Dallas—Edward Allen, Michael McFarland, Don Snyder, and Peter Smith—decided to try their hand at pulling off a "country Woodstock" on a ranch in (at that time) out of the way Dripping Springs. Because it was a country event, the original intent was that it attract a very different audience, one full of the typically conservative, square, and almost family oriented music lover. The advertised line-up of stars reflected that idea as well, with country superstar Charlie Rich the "headliner," but also included Tom T. Hall, Dottie West, Roy Acuff and Sonny James. But it was scheduled to be a three day event, so minor and local acts also had to be booked, and that proved to be the most lasting element of the whole extravaganza.

Willie Nelson was not an advertised performer, and neither was Waylon Jennings, but both appeared and they encouraged their fans to turn out as well. The promoters of the event anticipated 200,000 to buy tickets and come to the festival, so the three-day crowd of less than 20,000 was a huge disappointment and a financial disaster. However, it was the ones who did come that had the impact. The fans of acts such as James, West, and Rich—those suburbanites who enjoyed the "Nashville Sound" had no intention of leaving their leafy environs and trekking to some box canyon in Dripping Springs, but those of Progressive country—the hippies, young people, and working class—came and enjoyed what they heard. And mostly what they enjoyed was Willie, Waylon, and the boys, not Sonny James.

The Dripping Springs festival may not have been the success that the promoters had hoped, but it did spawn an idea in the mind of one of the participants: Willie Nelson. Nelson took notice of the "non-traditional" fans in the audience that day, the ones who enjoyed hearing country music in a format usually reserved for rock acts. Also, the egalitarian spirit and individualism among many of those fans were exactly the type of audience that Willie had targeted with his move back to Texas. Nelson gave an indication of how he was thinking at the event when he was asked by a *Rolling Stone* reporter if he would attend such an event again. He replied, "You mean if the same people was running it, or somebody else was?"

Out of the Dripping Springs festival was born Willie Nelson's 4th of July picnic in 1973. Eddie Wilson, the owner of the iconic Armadillo World Headquarters, promoted the event, and it was held once again in the ranch canyon near Dripping Springs. Nelson recruited his friends and fellow Progressive Country performers Kris Kristofferson, Rita Coolidge, and Waylon Jennings, along with other acts, and he promoted the event to appeal not to the conservative listeners of the "Nashville Sound," but to hippies, working people, and those who, as he once said, "like to drink their beer from a can in a real honky-tonk." 50,000 fans jammed the canyon amphitheater, and despite heat strokes, a lack of sanitation and toilets, and poor security, it helped to germinate not just an event but the popularity of "Outlaw Country."

Willie expanded the picnic in 1974, when he held a three-day event at the Texas World Speedway near College Station. He was joined not only by usual Jennings, Kristofferson and Tom T. Hall, but also Michael Martin Murphy—the godfather of the "Cosmic Cowboy" movement—troubadour/beach bum Jimmy Buffett, and another musical refugee who landed in Texas, Jerry Jeff Walker. After that, Willie's picnic was established as an event, one that was to be held every year, a true Texas Independence Day tradition.

Do Fence Me In: Barbed Wire and the Texas Cattle Industry

ASK ANYONE—NATIVE OR NON-TEXAN—to draw a "Texan" and I'll wager that 99% of them will sketch a man with a wide brimmed, tall crowned hat, boots, jeans, spurs, and probably a six-shooter on his hip. Yes, to many a Texan is synonymous with the cowboy, and he in turn is indelibly allied with the state's ranching industry, and no state is more closely affiliated with cattle than Texas. While the cowboy image is probably most often celebrated as part of Texas' open-range ranching heritage, Texas' prominence as a cattle raising state—the business side of "cowboying"—owes more to the passing the open-range era than to that short romantic period so often portrayed in film and literature. Texas' rise as the nation's premier bovine producer is mostly due to the end of the open range, a demise largely brought about with the invention and wide-spread use of a specific kind of technology—the barbed wire fence.

When cattlemen in the 1870s first ventured onto the plains of Texas, the wide open spaces that were so conducive to the raising of stock, they found a place that seemed perfect for the accepted Spanish/Mexican tradition of the open-range. A man could round up thousands of South Texas bovines, those primary descendants of the Spanish breeds brought to Texas in the 1700s that had evolved into the legendary "Texas longhorn," and then simply let them loose upon the plains and allow them to feed and prosper on the natural buffalo grasses of the Texas plains. The Texas open range had become a reality.

The "Texas longhorn" of the late 19th century actually bore little resemblance to the longhorns of today. Instead, these were small, wiry, tough, feral cattle that had evolved in South Texas to protect themselves from predators, drought, and any conditions nature could throw at them. They were also not some beast genetically selected to produce high-grade beef. On the contrary, their meat was stringy, tough, and "gamey," a product that a discerning palate would probably call inedible. That did not matter in the 1870s because the teeming masses in the cities of the East wanted meat, and discerning was generally never used to describe their tastes in cuisine. For them, the Texas longhorn worked just fine. Open range cattle ranchers began to carve out a good existence on the West Texas plains.

Such a system worked just fine when hardly anyone lived in West Texas. Cattlemen could graze their herds on the open public lands, which meant there was no need to actually secure title to the range. A West Texas cattle raiser might buy (or claim) acres around a water source and a place to locate a headquarters building and pens, but there was no need for any more holdings. It was an economical system, one that allowed men of little means to become agricultural entrepreneurs.

The open-range system was economical, but it still had problems. One of those was efficiency. Open range stock could not be selectively bred, and the bovines could not be discerningly culled; stock that was ill-suited to meat production continued to breed and taint the herd through generations. The only way to solve that problem was through fencing. Barriers were also the preference of the migrants who followed the cattlemen—farmers. The open-range was anathema to those who cultivated the soil; unpinned cattle trampled and ate crops. The two agricultural pursuits could not co-exist without fences.

The problem was that fencing of the era was very expensive and not practical on the vast plains of West Texas. Stone and wood fences were the norm in East Texas, along with water-filled ditches, thick, planted hedges, and sod blockades. Stone large enough to build fencing was scarce in West Texas, and wood was almost non-existent. Even if those had been plentiful, the labor and expense to enclose thousands of acres, and given the scarcity of water and foliage on the plains that was the size of the ranches, was prohibitive. Thus, West Texas ranches faced two problems: population and town building depended on the establishment of farms, and selective beef breeds needed enclosure, but economics trumped such solutions.

Everything began to change in 1874. In that year, Joseph Glidden of Illinois gained a patent for a new fencing material, a series of sharp points wrapped around a single strand of wire that would eventually come to be known as "barbed wire." The new material would prove perfect for the plains cattle industry. Barbed wire salesman began to sell miles of their strands to Texas ranchers, particularly after a famous demonstration of its effectiveness in holding a pen of cattle on Alamo Plaza in San Antonio. When large operations such as Charles Goodnight's JA and the famed XIT began to enclose their holdings the die was cast—"the Devil's rope" would become the preferred fencing material of cattle ranchers.

The invention of barbed wire changed Texas' cattle industry. Cattlemen could now buy and gain title to huge tracts of land, which would give them clear grazing rights to develop herds. Also, they could now stock the fenced range with breeds specifically engineered as beef cattle, which ended the reign of the longhorn and ushered in the age of the Hereford, Angus, and other beef cattle. Farms could find their place on the plains, and that would lead to towns, which would bring the railroad, which then helped to end the era of the cattle drive. Ranchers became more prosperous, and West Texas grew in population, and much of it was because of a cheap strand of wire studded with barbs. Sometimes, history turns on things that seem inconsequential at the time.

Baseball in Texas

I AM A BASEBALL MAN. I enjoy almost all sports—I have even grudgingly began to enjoy soccer—but it seems that baseball is the one that I am most fond of. I played a little baseball, but get the most satisfaction out of watching, analyzing, and discussing the nation's pastime, an activity that seems to grow more enjoyable as I age. Perhaps it is the slow nature of the game, or perhaps it is the almost "scientific" strategy of the sport that attracts me, but when the calendar turns to spring, my interest turns to the pastoral sport. So, for the next few weeks I would like to examine some of the great baseball players and teams Texas has produced, but first a little primer on baseball in the state.

Baseball in Texas began, perhaps appropriately, with a final score that looked more like a modern football game instead of a baseball contest. As part of San Jacinto Day (April 21), 1867, the Houston Stonewalls—who had formed a team almost a year earlier but had not yet played an official game—beat the Galveston Robert E. Lee's, organized just for the occasion, by the score of 35-2. The majority of the Stonewall players were occupying Union soldiers (which probably explains the Galveston team's name), men who had brought baseball to the South. Baseball was a northern game until after the Civil War, but one positive aspect we can take from that terrible fight, other than it ending slavery, was that it spread baseball throughout the nation.

It didn't take long for the game to proliferate. Union soldiers all over East Texas taught the game to residents, and then northern railroad workers played the game during lulls in construction of the rail lines across the state. Before long, almost every town and city in the state fielded their own team, and play became sources of community rivalry, as well as part of civic pride. The Fort Worth Cats became a powerhouse and the Houston Buffaloes did as well, which given their size was to be expected, but even small town teams could form formidable squads. The Alpine Bucks, from far West Texas, for example, became one of the best teams in the state, often crushing opponents from much larger municipalities.

Businesses helped the game to grow as businessmen discovered that baseball could be a way to promote a product or help to move into a market. These entrepreneurs financed and formed many of the civic and company teams, and they recruited and paid good players—technically they worked for the parent company—to do nothing but play baseball. These games could produce some lopsided and unbelievable outcomes. The Corsicana Oil City team, financed by Corsicana oil men, once beat the Texarkana Casketmakers (guess which business they represented) 51-3. A Corsicana player in that game belted eight home runs.

When professional baseball grew in the late 19th century and into the early 20th, Texas became the home of more minor league teams than any other state. The Texas League, which still exists as a AA circuit, was formed in 1888, and Texas also became the home of many D, C, and B league teams as well. The West Texas/New Mexico League, formed in the 1920s, gained the reputation as one of the strongest "D" leagues in the nation. A descendant of that alliance was the Longhorn League, and in 1955 Joe Baughman, a player for the Alpine Cowboys, hit an all-time record 72 home runs in a single season.

An MLB team finally arrived in Texas in 1964 with the Houston Colt 45's, who are now the Houston Astros. They were joined by the Texas Rangers, who moved to Arlington in 1972 from Washington D.C. and changed their name from the Senators. They play in multi-million dollar facilities and field teams that are a far cry from those town teams of old. But it is still the same game, the one that Walt Whitman once called "our game—the American game," and it still captures the heart of some of us. Maybe it is as simple as this: Football—a Texas religion—stirs the emotional, almost guttural side of many people, but baseball satisfies the logical, reasonable side, or at least it does to those of us who love it, or that is what we tell ourselves!

Casting a Hooded Shadow Across the Land: Texas and the 2nd Ku Kux Klan

WHENEVER MOST PEOPLE COME ACROSS a picture of a man in a white robe and a hood with only eye holes cut into it they shudder and get the impression of a racist organization that operates on the fringes of society and deals primarily in fear and intimidation. To me, they have always been the ultimate bullies who hide behind a mask while spewing their message of hate. Certainly today the Klan is not a part of the mainstream of society or politics, and those associated with the Klan face certain ostracism from most of society. But, can you imagine a time when the Klan was an accepted and open part of our society? When prominent members of communities openly claimed KKK membership? When even someone as prominent as a senator was a Ku Klux Klan member. Shockingly, such a time was not that long ago, and Texas, like a good portion of the rest of the nation, came under the large influence of the Klan during the 1920s.

There have been three incarnations of the Ku Klux Klan. The first Klan, and the group that gave it the unusual name, began when six Confederate veterans in Pulaski, Tennessee began a secret vigilante group with the aim to fully restore white supremacy. The Reconstruction Republican federal government eventually put an end to this Klan in the early 1870s. The second KKK rose in Georgia in 1915, although they did not really spread outside that state until the 1920s. This Klan retained the racist and jingoistic policies of its predecessors, but used the specter of modernity and increasing urbanity to make their movement more widespread.

The second Klan spread by closely organizing as a fraternal group, but also by decrying the rapid changes taking place throughout the nation in the 1920s. The "invisible empire," as Klansmen often referred to their group, came to Texas in September 1920 when a kleagle, the Klan equivalent of a recruiter, and made their pitch during a Confederate veterans meeting. He found a receptive audience, and who he successfully recruited is symbolic of how and why the 2nd KKK was the most successful of the three versions. The first Klan was largely limited to, "unreconstructed Confederates" and mostly drew from a rural, almost working class constituency. The third "Klan," which is more of a relationship between various white supremacist groups that began during the civil rights era and continues today, draw most of their members from the "lower orders" of society. But in Houston the recruiter's message resonated with bankers, business owners, and professionals. The second Klan was much more mainstream.

The Texas Klan quickly spread to almost every major city in the state, and by 1923 boasted more than 150,000 members. Many members justified their membership as a business necessity since it recruited so many prominent members; others claimed that they did not wholly agree with the group's hateful rhetoric and actions toward African Americans and other ethnic groups, but joined and supported the racist cabal because it represented a "restoration of old, rural values of decency and honesty." Certainly, the 2nd Klan used such homilies to recruit members and present a more presentable public image, but the reality was that at its core it was still the same racist, regressive organization it had been fifty years earlier.

The 2nd KKK often participated in charity and other benevolent events during the day, and held peaceful marches on holidays and other solemn occasions, but its nocturnal and private activities reflected its true nature. KKK members attacked a Dallas bellhop because he was suspected of having a sexual relationship with a white woman. He was beaten and his forehead branded with KKK. The Klan was suspected (and most evidence pointed to Klansmen) in at least ten murders of blacks men in Houston in 1922. They also beat and tarred and feathered a woman in Tenaha simply because some questioned whether she had divorced before she married again. One man was flogged to death for the offense of speaking German in public. None of these cases resulted in any prosecution, and in many instances those responsible for arresting and trying such actors were Klansmen themselves.

The Klan boasted of its influence when it openly helped to elect Earle Mayfield to the senate in 1922, and they set their eyes on the governor's mansion in 1924. They made a coalition with some other groups and unified behind Dallas judge Felix Robertson. It looked as if they would win the election until impeached former governor James E. Ferguson entered the arena. Ferguson was forbidden to run for governor again due to his impeachment conviction, but nothing could prevent him placing his wife, Miriam, on the ballot. The Ferguson's trumped the Klan by openly challenging their violent and exclusionary nature, while also utilizing the same populist message that had worked so well for James in 1915 and 1917. In the end, Mrs. Ferguson beat Robertson in a run-off.

The defeat precipitated a decline for the Klan, and by 1926 anti-Klan sentiment reached critical mass. The legislature passed an "anti-mask" law that was directly targeted at the hooded racists, and prosecutors and law enforcement began to charge and try Klansmen suspected of criminal activity. While the Klan continued to press their agenda in the next few years, they were thwarted at most levels, which culminated in 1928 when Mayfield lost his re-election bid. Klan influence waned to near nothing, but it is frightening to think that they came so close to taking over the state during this era.

Cinco de Mayo and the "Texas Connection"

CINCO DE MAYO IS THOUGHT BY MANY to be one of the most important and widely celebrated Mexican holidays. The reality is that while it once was more widely celebrated in Mexico, today its celebration is largely confined to the state of Puebla, and that it is a much more lively commemoration in the United States, particularly in Texas. Which is only natural since while the day celebrates a Mexican victory over French invasion troops at the Battle of Puebla in 1862, the leader and hero of that monumental battle was a Texan, Ignacio Zaragoza.

General Ignacio Seguin Zaragoza, was born on March 24, 1829 at La Bahia near present day Goliad, Zaragoza was a relative of Texas hero Juan Seguin. His father, Miguel Zaragoza, was a soldier of the garrison at La Bahia, but also a political supporter of the federalist faction in Coahuila that opposed Santa Anna and his regime that took power in Mexico in 1832. Despite his federalist leanings, the elder Zaragoza was a soldier first who remained loyal to the Mexican army, so when the Texas Revolution ended with Texas' independence he moved his family first to Matamoros and then on to Monterrey in 1844.

When the U.S./Mexican War began in 1846, Ignacio Zaragoza tried to join the officer corps of the Mexican Army but was rejected. He then opened up a store in Monterrey, but by 1853 was a part of the Nuevo Leon militia. Eventually, Zaragoza moved up the ranks and when his militia regiment became a part of the Mexican Army in the late 1850s, he attained the rank of captain.

Zaragoza became an unabashed supporter of the federalist forces who wished to establish a fully republican and democratic Mexico in the years following the U.S./Mexican War, and fought against the centralist forces of Santa Anna at the Battles of Saltillo and Monterrey. Mexico went through another period of conflict during the War of Reform (1857-1860), and Zaragoza fought with and came to the attention of liberal leader Benito Juarez.

Juarez appointed Zaragoza as his minister of war and navy in April 1861. Juarez moved to enact reforms in Mexico, and also remove European influence in Mexican society and in the nation's economy. Such moves led first the Spanish and later the English and French navies to sail to Mexico's waters to threaten Juarez's government. The Spanish and the English eventually withdrew, but the French continued to make invasion threats against Mexico. Zaragoza resigned his cabinet post to take command of the Army of the East in February 1862, and he traveled to the city of Puebla to prepare a defense against a potential French invasion.

The French attack did come on May 5, 1862. French commanders expected to quickly defeat the Mexican troops and make a march to Mexico City, but instead Zaragoza'a army dealt the invaders a monumental defeat. The battle lasted all day, and in the end the Mexican troops forced the complete withdrawal of the French. It is still considered one of the most decisive, and unexpected, defeats in world military history. Zaragoza was a hero throughout the nation, and upon his arrival in Mexico City he was given a parade and many accolades. He returned to his post at Puebla in late August 1862, but was quickly stricken with typhoid, which took his life on September 8. Benito Juarez immediately issued a proclamation declaring *Cinco de Mayo* a national holiday. The little boy who grew up near Goliad, Texas had entered the pantheon of Mexican heroes. It should remind us all that Texas and Mexico share more than a border—they share an intertwined heritage and a legacy that overlaps any political boundary.

Creating Their Own Space: Freedom Colonies

SLAVERY OFFICIALLY ENDED IN TEXAS when General Gordon Granger landed in Galveston on June 19, 1865 and read a declaration that "from this day forward all the bounds between bondsmen and masters are severed." Texas' slaves celebrated as only a people who have had a life-long prayer answered can, but for the vast majority they carried no outward grudge and only hoped that the society that had formerly kept them bound would now allow them to be independent and live a life of freedom.

That was the hope, but the reality turned out to be much different. Almost immediately the white supremacist power structure set about to restore their bi-racial society, but they had to do so without the mechanism of slavery. Former slave owners, with the full cooperation of social, economic, and political leaders, began to construct just such a structure through sharecropping, debt peonage, as well as "black codes," which restricted the political and social freedom of the former slaves. The Freedmen's dreams were shattered.

In the midst of such a hostile racial climate the former slaves became determined to use every means necessary to escape the grips of the racist southern society. Those that could often left the Texas and the South entirely, quite often moving to the West but also to the growing cities of the North and East. Most African Americans did not have the means to move great distances so they devised another way of escape: "Freedom Colonies."

Also called Freedman's Settlements, these colonies were in the rural countryside. The former slaves formed their own independent communities where they could farm, live, and worship in their own manner—and also away from the oppressive eyes and ears of a white society determined to reattach the former shackles of bondage. These were hardly ever "officially recognized" communities, and they were almost all unincorporated. Their bonds of unity came from the schools, churches, and homes that functioned as a cultural place of refuge for a people hungry for independence and freedom.

Freedman's colonies had to quite often make do on marginal land— "up in the sandhills" as some put it, but also in flood prone river bottoms, patches of scrub brush, or tangled, knotted wilderness areas that were difficult to clear and even more arduous to cultivate. But they made it work, and black ownership of land soared in Texas from just 1.8% of the population to over 30% by 1900, with the vast majority of the holdings within the confines of these "Freedom Colonies."

Some of these colonies were just places of residences for dispersed former slaves; others came together when church congregations moved en masse to the countryside. Still others, such as County Line, which is now known as Upshaw, in Nacogdoches County were settled by extended members of a single family. Whatever the means of establishment, they proved successful as by 1900 there were over three hundred of these communities dispersed throughout the eastern half of Texas.

Freedmen's settlements became a source of pride among African Texans, and they tenaciously held onto their land and their culture. In a time when whites in Texas and the South used numerous means to subjugate and even destroy black ways of life, these colonies became a means of preservation, places where African American culture not only survived but thrived. But small rural communities, no matter their origin, are often no match for the march of time and "progress," and by the 1920s these communities began to disappear. Younger African Texans left the settlements for the economic lure of the big cities, and at the same time crop prices and other commodities crucial to the survival of a rural life began to decline. The crucible of the Great Depression, followed by the upheaval of World War II for all practical purposes ended the "Freedom Colonies," although some do survive into the twenty-first century, a testament to the steadfast determination of a people who did all in their power to resist oppression and build an independent life for future generations.

Saving a Texas Shrine

FOR MOST AMERICANS, MARCH IS THE SIGNAL month for the beginning of spring and a time for renewal. Texans like spring as well (although East Texans know March as the "arrival of the green snow"), but for them March also means remembrances of the Texas Revolution and its symbols such as San Jacinto, Stephen F. Austin, Sam Houston, and of course, The Alamo. The little mission church and partial "long barracks" in downtown San Antonio has become an iconic symbol of Texas. The Alamo as a badge of Texas honor is somewhat ironic, given the fact that at the turn of the twentieth century Texans seemed to be ready to allow that little chapel and what was left of its other buildings rot away and be lost to posterity, and they would have had it not been for the purposeful efforts the Daughters of the Republic of Texas (DRT), and the iron will of two special DRTs, Clara Driscoll and Adina de Zavala.

In the years immediately following the Texas Revolution the mission of San Antonio de Valero was treated with anything but reverence. San Antonioians felt no guilt in taking the limestone blocks, timbers, and other materials from the old Spanish structure to use in their building projects. All of the outer walls vanished, and other edifices inside those walls crumbled and disintegrated. When Texas became part of the United States, all that was left of the site of the famous battle was the dilapidated old chapel and a part of the old convent, known during the battle as the Long Barracks.

The United States Army occupied what was left of the Alamo for a while, but no one really knew who actually owned the chapel, although a local merchant was using it as his warehouse. Eventually the ownership question went to a courtroom, which decided that the Archdiocese of San Antonio owned what was left of the church—but only the chapel—and the rest of the mostly vacant land surrounding it was sold to private interests. The old convent was sold to the wholesale grocery firm of Hugo & Schmeltzer. The state of Texas did buy the chapel from the Catholic Church, but through the 1890s they did very little with it.

Thus by the dawn of the twentieth century, what we know today as the Alamo was a crumbling mess, an eyesore in the center of San Antonio. Perhaps the state and its citizens would have realized the folly of not preserving this vital piece of history, but given its track record at the time perhaps not. Clara Driscoll and Adina de Zavala were two people who did believe fervently in saving the old mission. They were members of a patriotic women's group that had formed in 1891, the Daughters of the Republic of Texas (DRT). Driscoll and de Zavala—who would later wage their own personal battle over the Alamo—combined their talents to eventually bring the Alamo under the control of the DRT and save it for future generations.

Adina de Zavala was the granddaughter of Lorenzo de Zavala, a signer of the Texas declaration of independence and the first (interim) Vice-President of the Republic. De Zavala joined a group of preservationist and civic minded San Antonio women in 1889, a group that became one of the first groups to coalesce into the Daughters of the Republic of Texas in 1891. She became committed to preserving the Alamo, and as early as 1892 had convinced Hugo & Schmeltzer to allow her organization to buy the Long Barracks and other grounds if they ever had a mind to sell.

Clara Driscoll was a child of South Texas; her father owned and operated a successful ranch in Nueces County where Clara grew up in the lap of luxury. She studied and traveled extensively in Europe as a young woman, and grew fond of the way European cities preserved their historic sites as parks and places of reverence. When she returned to Texas in 1899, she decided to join the campaign to save the Alamo. She began to travel the state to raise funds to buy any available lands and buildings associated with the iconic mission.

Driscoll joined the DRT in 1903, and along with de Zavala began a more concentrated campaign to save the Alamo. They approached Hugo & Schmaltzer about buying the Long Barracks and some vacant land just north of the chapel. The wholesalers quoted what they thought was an outrageous price of $75,000, but Drsicoll, de Zavala, and the DRT set about to raise the funds. They lobbied the Texas legislature for $5,000 to option the purchase, and although the legislature appropriated the money, Governor S.W.T. Lanham vetoed the measure. Clara Driscoll then paid the entire $5,000 out of her own pocket.

One year later, the DRT fundraising efforts remained woefully short, but once again Clara Driscoll rescued the project. She paid Hugo & Schmaltzer a $20,000 payment they had demanded to keep the option to buy the land, and she also personally secured loans to pay the remainder of the purchase. The project was alive, but Clara Dcoll was on the hook for the entire amount.

Perhaps it was the spunky fight these patriotic women put up that changed some minds. Maybe Texans just love an underdog. Whatever the reason, the fund raising campaign gained momentum. Money came in from throughout the state, and legislators and county officials rushed to make the campaign to save the Alamo a political issue. When the Texas legislature met in January 1905, one of their first actions was to appropriate $65,000 to complete the purchase from Hugo & Schmaltzer. At the same time, the state turned over custodianship of the chapel, as well as all the grounds, to the DRT.

For over a hundred years, the DRT made good on their promise and preserved, maintained, and operated the site. The Alamo, as we know it today, became a place of reflection and reverence, just as the plucky women of the early twentieth century envisioned. Recently, in a controversial move, the state of Texas took back control of the shrine from the DRT. It remains to be seen if they will be the same worthy caretakers.

The Origin of Tex-Mex

ANYONE WHO KNOWS ME (or has had the occasion to view me in the flesh) understands that I have a special relationship with food. The simple fact is—I love it. Let me temper that with a codicil in case my doctor is reading this: I am overcoming my amorous relationship with vittles and have not gone off my diet. Just allow me my paean to past indulgences. I have tasted and studied foods of all kinds and varieties, but no matter how far I stray from my roots, the one dish that I always come back to and continue to have longing pangs for is what most Texans call "Mexican food," but in reality is Tex-Mex.

Tex-Mex is a specific variety of food, a combination of the preferred dishes of Spanish/Mexican recipes combined with Anglo American preferences. While the actual preparation and varieties of the food began in the nineteenth century, the first verifiable appearance of the term "Tex-Mex" was not until the 1940s, although it did not become "official" until 1972 when food critics and cookbook authors began referring to Americanized Mexican food as "Tex-Mex."

So what exactly is it? Its true origin is as a frontier food enjoyed within the reaches of what is now northern Mexico. Those hardy settlers in Chihuahua, Coahuila, and Tamaulipas, began to combine some key ingredients such as beans, corn, chili peppers, and tortillas with whatever other foods they had on hand to develop a specific food. It was these recipes that became staples across what is now South Texas between Brownsville and San Antonio.

Good food travels, and the simple fare of South Texas migrated northward with the *vaqueros* and the cattle herds of the mid- to late

1800s. Anglo Americans, when introduced to what they called "Mexican food," began putting their own stamp on the variety, adding beef, melted cheddar cheese, chili con carne, and fried tortilla chips to create the familiar forms of Tex-Mex such as nachos, tacos, chalupas, fajitas, and of course chili.

The cuisine went mainstream in the 1950s with the rise in popularity of the "Mexican Restaurant," quite often owned and/or operated by recent Mexican immigrants who cooked and served good, simple, relatively cheap fare for the growing populations in Texas, New Mexico, Arizona, and California. The Mexican kitchens made most of their menu very simply: combination plates of enchiladas, tacos, and chalupas combined with rice and refried beans. Eventually, new creations such as chimichangas and fajitas were added to the menu, but they all had common features: yellow cheese, tortillas, salsa, and chili gravy which all evolved as the foundation of Tex-Mex. Most importantly, it was reasonably priced, a food of the working and lower-middle class.

Like all things, too much success means too many people begin to mess with a good thing. Such has become the case with Tex-Mex. Many restaurants, probably due to the desire to offer "healthy alternatives," are putting recipes on their menu that are not authentic Tex-Mex. Today, you can find "chicken nachos," which are certainly an affront to any Tex-Mex cook worth their salt. Don't get me started on such monstrosities as "shrimp fajitas" or "vegetarian chili" (who in the world thought it was a good idea to develop a meatless chili? If it has no meat, it is not chili. And you had better not put any beans in my chili either). I was once in Santa Fe and a well-known restaurant there served me enchiladas made with blue corn tortillas, asadero cheese, and black beans. They then had the audacity to charge me over $20.00 for such a mess. I think that I will just stick to a combination plate #1, and go heavy on the chili gravy, please.

The Myth of Reconstruction in Texas

THE LEGACY OF RECONSTRUCTION IN TEXAS is one with a mixed legacy. The presence of federal troops in the state, which caused great consternation among most whites in the state, did provide—if only briefly—the opportunity for African Texans to finally receive a semblance of citizenship, as well as demonstrate that they were capable of discharging those responsibilities and make remarkable progress, especially given their centuries long condition of oppression and bondage. However, when it finally ended, the Texas government once again returned to the hands of the same men who had led it out of the Union in 1860, leaders who would become known as the "Redeemers" because their primary goal was to restore Texas once again to a social organization dominated by the concept of white superiority, the same philosophy that had ultimately led to secession.

Another curious attitude also developed within the first few decades after the end of Reconstruction, the construction of a mythical past that has persisted into the present. No sooner had it ended that Texans began to categorize the presence of federal troops and Republican government as the most dastardly period ever in the state's period, perhaps rivaled only by Santa Anna's Mexico. This interpretation insisted that Reconstruction was a time when Texans were terrorized by not only federal troops, but black State Policemen who had little regard for the law. The federals allowed "Carpetbaggers" to infiltrate the state and take over the government and the economy and run Texas like a corrupt regime just for their benefit. Whites were seriously oppressed and those same Carpetbaggers and Republicans allowed illiterate blacks who were recently slaves to participate in such corruption. Only the saviors known as the "Redeemers" were able to restore order.

Such an interpretation became the only accepted narrative of Reconstruction for the majority of Texans. As late as the 1990s, a newspaper article wrote that "Reconstruction lined the pockets. . . .of Carperbaggers, [and]. . .left. . .Texans broke and bitter." Unfortunately, such an interpretation has little basis in fact. Carpetbaggers ran Texas? Recent transplants from the North comprised fewer than one-quarter of the seats in the state and county governments under Republican governor Edmund J. Davis. In terms of the economy, and the idea that most of the wealthy elite in Texas lost their fortunes during the period, that is also false. They did lose their slaves, but over 90% retained their land, and a good portion of those obtained more—quite often at the expense of smaller land holders who "blamed" their loss on those dreaded Carpetbaggers. Generally, they remained where they always were—wealthier than almost all Texans. As for the presence of federal troops, records show that or the most part they avoided interactions with the public, and behaved unlike any occupying army has ever acted in any time. The State Police? Almost all the violent encounters between them and the citizens they served were initiated by white Texans angry that freedmen were placed in positions of authority. The vast majority of violence in the state during Reconstruction was inflicted upon freedmen and former Unionists by the Ku Klux Klan, as well as the reigniting of old feuds that flamed due to a lack of effective law enforcement.

In the end, this myth was carefully constructed to draw attention away from the actual intent—restore the bi-racial social organization that, had existed under slavery. It was demagoguery at its best: find a narrative that blames a scapegoat that allows the supposed aggrieved party to avoid its true actions. Federal Reconstruction was actually a fairly benign process, and one that proceeded much faster—and more fair— than most ever anticipated.

The Sad Saga of Felix Longoria

WHEN MOST PEOPLE THINK OF JIM CROW, segregation, and inequality in Texas their first thought, understandably, is the dreadful treatment of African Texans under the system of white superiority endemic of the American South. Many overlook that just as significant, and just as shameful, were the oppressive practices inflicted upon Tejanos during the same period. One of the most disgraceful events directed toward Texans of Mexican descent was the Felix Longoria Affair in Three Rivers, Texas in 1948.

Like many Tejanos when World War II began, Felix Longoria proudly volunteered for service in the United States Army. Longoria served with distinction throughout his tenure, and in the final days of the war he volunteered once again, this time to be a part of a dangerous mission against one of the last remnants of Japanese defenses in the Philippines. Longoria fell during the mission, but his body was never identified and recovered.

After World War II the United States military began to try to recover and return as soldiers lost during overseas battles. Longoria's remains were recovered in 1948 and returned to his family in Three Rivers, where they began to prepare him for burial. Three Rivers, like many Texas cities, had a segregated cemetery and in that South Texas city Longoria was slated to be buried in the "Mexican" section. As abominable as that sounds, the fact that custom would segregate people even in death, the situation deteriorated further for the Longorias when the director of the cemetery (who was also the town's only funeral director) refused the use of the burial ground's chapel for the service of the fallen soldier. His explanation? "Whites wouldn't like it," he said, and that "Mexicans had created trouble at previous funerals."

Frustrated, angry, and probably perplexed at such a reaction, Longoria's family turned to a new Mexican American advocacy organization, the American G.I. Forum, and its founder and director Dr. Hector P. Garcia. Latinos had fought and died in numbers far greater than the percentage of their population during World War II, but when they returned they found they still faced discrimination and oppression, and also were denied many of the benefits promised through the G.I. Bill of Rights passed in 1944. Garcia organized the Forum to press for those rights and to fight discrimination.

Garcia and the Forum first chose to meet with the funeral director and appeal to his sense of decency and patriotism, but received the same negative response. The Forum next began to protest the action, but that led to no action as well. Garcia then contacted new Texas senator Lyndon B. Johnson to ask for aid, and Johnson tried to broker a compromise, but the funeral director—backed by the white power structure of the city—refused to accommodate the request. Johnson then made arrangements to have Longoria buried at Arlington National Cemetery, where he was interred with full military honors.

The controversy led the Texas House of Representatives to make an investigation, and a five-member special committee held hearings, interviewed participants, and issued a report. Their conclusion baffled Longoria's family and Dr. Garcia. Four of the five committee members concluded that while the funeral director's actions were unfortunate, he had not acted out of a discriminatory policy and had no malice toward the Longorias (a fifth member did not sign the report because he believed the actions to be explicit discrimination). The committee report was symbolic of the larger barrier to any movement on racial and ethnic discrimination: because the system was so entrenched, was so much a part of the everyday lives of white Texans, they simply could not see how oppressive and reprehensible such discriminatory actions could be. It would be many years, many tears, and many battles before our state would even begin to correct such wrongs. For the Longorias it came too late, but their persistence helped pave the way for future generations to receive greater equality.

What Was Sam Houston's Ultimate Plan?

ONE OF THE MOST ENJOYABLE THINGS about being a historian involves the opportunity to engage in some pure speculation, an analytical look at facts and evidence to try to answer a question such as "what was he/she thinking?" Some of the most intriguing questions in our past involve actions during a war, and the Texas Revolution provides many chances to speculate, wonder, and very often scratch one's head in complete disbelief. Perhaps the most frequent of those questions involves Sam Houston and the Texas Army's retreat across Texas in the months after the fall of the Alamo. Many people have offered possibilities, but still the questions remains: What was Sam Houston's plan?

After initial victories in 1835 over the small Mexican forces in Texas at Gonzales and San Antonio, the Texian rebels had encountered the full force of Mexican President Santa Anna's forces as his large army swept up out of the interior of Mexico. One detachment of the Mexican forces under General Jose Urrea had moved more to the east as they marched across the Rio Grande; he would defeat Texian forces at San Patricio and Agua Dulce before moving on to crush James W. Fannin's troops at Coleto Creek.

Santa Anna had led another, larger body north to San Antonio and the siege and eventual battle at the Alamo. After laying waste to the mission fortress, Santa Anna split this army sending one group under General Antonio Gaona northeast toward Nacogdoches and East Texas, while he stayed with another detachment that would move out of San Antonio toward Gonzales and San Felipe de Austin.

The Convention at Washington-on-the-Brazos had confirmed Sam Houston's position as General of the Texas Army, but in early

March 1836 Houston had no army to command and he now had to quickly raise a force. During the weeks after the March 2 independence convention Houston did raise a fairly sizable force, but he faced a quandary about how to proceed. The defenders of the Alamo had ignored Houston's requests to abandon the mission and move east, which had cost them their lives; James W. Fannin dallied too long in moving out of Goliad, which made him an easy target for Urrea. Thus Houston's force remained the lone Texian military detachment in the region, the only troops who could confront the large Mexican armies. Should he directly attack the main force immediately and then hope to win a victory and fight the other two forces at a later time? Or should he try to hold out and fight when he had a chance to win? When would that be?

Houston chose to retreat, but, where was he headed? If one looks at the direction he took it seems as if he was marching almost directly toward Nacogdoches, East Texas, and the Sabine River. Many of his troops (and President Burnet) accused Houston of cowardice, but is it possible that he had a very definite intent? The answer may lie in what Houston had done in February 1836 and the actions of many of the men of Nacogdoches, although a definitive answer will never be known because Houston kept his own counsel.

The Consultation of January 1836 had named Sam Houston the commander of the Texas Army, and had then commissioned the new general to raise his own army. Instead of immediately proceeding with such a task Houston took a furlough and went to Nacogdoches and East Texas, where he remained throughout February. Presumably Houston's intent in East Texas was to treat with the Cherokee to make sure they stayed out of the fight between the Texians and Santa Anna's army, and Houston did secure some kind of agreement with Duwali and the Cherokee to that end, but did it take the entire month to reach an arrangement with the Cherokee? Did Sam Houston have some other dealings in Nacogdoches?

When the Texas Army had called for volunteers in March some East Texans had responded to the request, but just as many remained in their homes and settlements; such actions even created a controversy as some Texians in the rest of the region accused the East Texans of not supporting the cause or pursuing some independent course of action. But what if Sam Houston had asked the men of East Texas to stay because his intention was to lead the Mexican army into the forests and the Redlands to make his stand? After all, the Mexican armies would have to cross large rivers to get to East Texas, and the natural cover and forests would lessen the Mexican numerical advantage. Also, Houston knew that American General Edmund Pendleton Gaines had a large force at Fort Jessup just over the Sabine and that Andrew Jackson believed that all of Texas east of the Neches belonged to the United States. Might Gaines' men join the Texians in fighting the Mexicans in East Texas?

Of course, none of that happened. Santa Anna divided his army a third time, which gave Houston the opportunity to pursue and defeat him at San Jacinto. Texas' independence would then take the course we know today, but what if the last battle of the Revolution had occurred in East Texas? What would the course of our state's history have been then? It is fun to speculate.

Yes, We Were "Cowboys," Too

ASK ANYONE, ANYWHERE, FROM TEXARKANA to Tokyo, or from Bar Harbour, Maine to Bali to draw a Texan and I would be willing to bet a large amount that most of them would sketch a cowboy. It does not matter that the era of the traditional "cowboy" lasted just a little more than a decade, or that the cowboy image that Texans—and others—traditionally picture bears little actual resemblance to those men who worked on the ranches and on the trail drives of the late nineteenth century. The contemporary image of the cowboy is largely a construction of popular culture, a figure who owes its existence first to the "pulp novels" of the late nineteenth and early twentieth century, and then most spectacularly to Hollywood. The "western" genre of film has so ingrained the cowboy image on the American psyche that no amount of scholarship or commentary will ever diminish it. However, one thing that Hollywood got very incorrect, and because of its ubiquity it became entrenched, is that the cowboy was almost always a white man. If we are speaking of the actual historical cowboy, the men who filled the jobs on ranches, on drives, and in feedlots or other holding pens for stock, historical records prove that at least one-third—and perhaps more—of those workers were men of African descent (another one-third of these men were of Mexican ancestry). These black cowboys have been overlooked by much of traditional and popular historical accounts, even though they have been a part of Texas history since the "invention" of the cowboy.

The majority of the first black "cowboys" were slaves. Historical scholarship is increasingly uncovering the fact that a good many slave owners in Texas, particularly those out on the blackland prairie near the western frontier, used slaves as drovers and tenders of livestock. Like whites in the rest of Texas, these slaves utilized the stock raising techniques that came first from Spain and then filtered up to Texas through Mexico from the *vaqueros* that operated large ranches in South Texas. They tended stock not in the English/Scottish tradition of shepherding on foot and using dogs, but on horseback. In fact, the symbiotic relationship between man and horse that became perfected in Mexico and then came to Texas meant that a proper cowboy never dismounted while working, even eating or taking a nap in the saddle if the need rose.

After the Civil War and the end of slavery, many of these former slaves, as well as other Freedmen, found that they could avoid some—not all—of the restrictions, oppression, and hardships of "black code" Texas by leaving the eastern environs of the state and moving west. They found work as many did on the open range, as either drovers on the cattle drives or as "hands" on the region's nascent ranches. Those who had previously worked with cattle as slaves became the "ranch hands," as they were much too valuable to send up the trail on the cattle drives. African American cowboys became particularly prized on ranches for their ability to break horses as many gained a reputation as having some innate quality for such a job. That innate quality likely was patience and perseverance, skills that came in handy when one lived in either slavery or in a society that regarded you as a second class citizen.

Many of the black cowboys who worked on ranches and went on drives eventually became ranch foreman and managers, and even operated large ranches of their own. Others became trusted confidants and treasured aides to some of the most famous white cattlemen of the era. For example, Bose Ikard proved to be such a top hand that Charles Goodnight took the then unprecedented action of paying Ikard the same wages he did any "top hand" on his ranch near Palo Duro Canyon in West Texas. You may have heard of Ikard without knowing it; he was the model for the "Deets" character in Larry McMurtry's *Lonesome Dove*.

African Americans continued working in the ranching and stock industry into the twentieth century. Today, the "black cowboy" is finally getting some of his due in scholarship and even in film. That's fitting in my mind since it lets everyone know that they were part of the American lore of the cowboy, too.